Simply Celebrating Children

Parties As Unique & Special As A Child

By Dale Wipff Reinhard

Illustrated by Karen Rubio

Printed and bound in the United States of America
Library of Congress Catalog Number: 91-90169
ISBN 0-9628888-0-X

For information address:
Pressed Duck Publishing
Fort Sutter Station
P.O. Box 160931
Sacramento, California 95816-0931
1-800-523-DUCK

The author has tried to insure that all activities, games and refreshments detailed in the book are safe as well as entertaining. However, it is recommended by the author that **children be under adult supervision at all times**.

Cover, author sketch and interior illustrations by Karen Rubio
Graphic codes by Lisa Bacchini

Special thanks to Cousin Josie, Dolly, Lanie, Michele,
Maryellen Burns of After The Fact,
Gini Alexander of Fong & Fong Printers and Lithographers,
Gene of Palmer Courier Service.
Thanks for technical advice and expertise to Bob Reinhard,
the staff of The Electric Page, and to Officewise Associates.

A portion of the profits from this book will be donated to the
Make A Wish Foundation

Dedication.....

to Mom & Dad . . .
for showing me how to celebrate life,

to Bob, Robert & Kelly . . .
for making each day a celebration,

to family & friends . . .
for their caring support,

This book truly celebrates you.

Dale

to Greg, Jeff & Emily.....

♡ Mue!

TABLE OF CONTENTS

ACTIVITY CODES

Lively Group

Quiet Group

See Page 2 For Details

GETTING YOUR FEET WET

How & Why To Use This Book

It is natural to feel a sense of panic at the thought of hosting a children's party. To willingly entertain a dozen or more children at a birthday party, classroom or club meeting is certainly not a normal, everyday occurrence. But then . . . **celebrations are not meant to be like any other day.**

What makes any occasion "magical" to a child is the joyful feeling of being "celebrated" . . . of being a **SHINING STAR** for a few hours.

Hopefully this book will encourage you to create lots of occasions to **celebrate children** throughout the year. Besides a birthday party at home, plan a classroom party at school, instant rainy day (or sunny day) activities, "cheer up" sick-in-bed days or just plain family "no occasion" celebrations!

Sometimes the best celebrations are ones without a reason.

Any party in the book can easily be altered to suit your child's interests. By interchanging, mixing and combining activities, you can create a party that is truly "**custom-made**" for your child. To help plan your special event, each party in the book has been divided into **five key elements**:

Invitations: unique ideas to build anticipation for the big event

Moodmakers: simple magic to turn ordinary household items into extraordinary decorations

Refreshments: imaginative ways to serve tasty treats

Activities: versatile games to entertain a variety of ages

Favors: unusual souvenirs for guests to take home

If you should already have a theme in mind but need entertainment ideas, **ACTIVITY CODES** have been devised so you can swiftly select those activities which best match the liveliness level of your group.

These marginal codes can be found in the **ACTIVITIES** section of every chapter.

There is also an **ACTIVITY INDEX** listing every activity by age and liveliness level of the children.

ACTIVITY CODES

QUIET GROUP

LIVELY GROUP

Become a child again yourself . . . if even for a few hours. There's no better way of **GETTING YOUR FEET WET** than to tap into your own "**natural resources**" and release your imagination. Try to include your child in the planning process. As you build a party around your child, you build your child's self-esteem at the same time.

Your extra efforts will silently say **you want a party to be as unique and special as your child**. Strangely enough, the best gift you give your child may actually be an <u>**invisible**</u> one . . . **a shared celebration with memories to last a lifetime.**

SET SAIL WITH DUCKLES

.............AND DISCOVER YOUR CHILD!

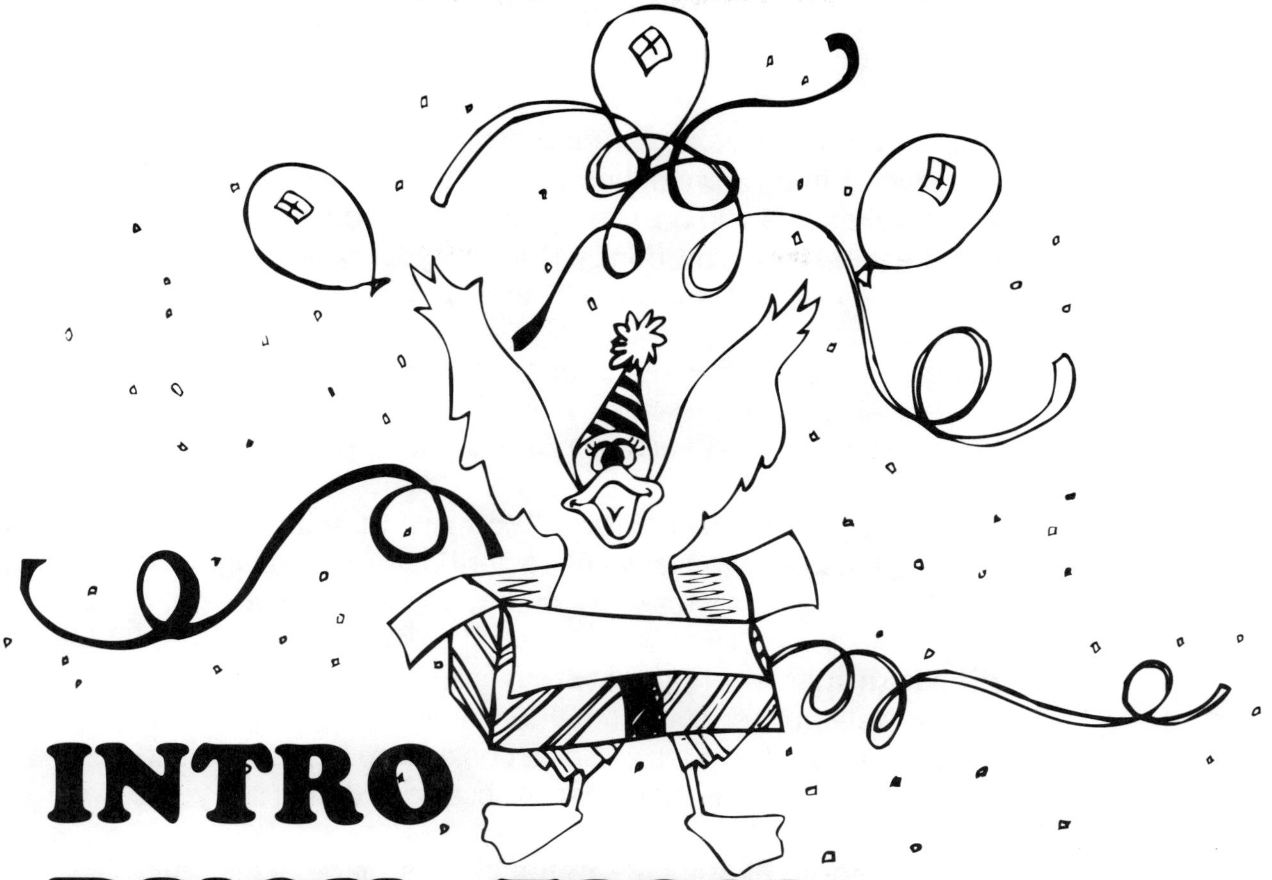

INTRO DUCK TION

Think Of The Complete Package

A party can be your best gift. Besides a yearly birthday, try to provide other occasions to place children in the spotlight. Even a large family can give each child the chance to be center stage and truly **celebrated** . . . if only for a few hours. Any date you choose can feel magical by interrupting the daily routine with an unexpected surprise:

- **Hang balloons and/or crepe paper** from a child's bedroom ceiling. Have a family chorus **singing alarm clock** wake the "celebration child" with a soft (or loud) rendition of the "Happy Birthday" song or another variation of the same tune with lyrics that repeat, "We Do Love You, We Do".

- **Place a trail of confetti, pennies or foil-wrapped candies** for a child to follow from his bedside to a birthday surprise package hidden in another room.

- **Write "Happy Birthday" or "We Love You" on the bathroom mirror** with toothpaste or shaving cream, then place surprise "You're Special" cards in any drawers he/she might open.

- Prepare a **quick treasure hunt** by writing several "clue cards" and placing them around the house. For example, your child might wake up to find a rhyming "clue card" on his/her pillow with the message, "Why don't you look in your shoe!" The final clue would direct your child to a surprise package or card.

- **Hang a large banner** made of newsprint (most newspaper offices sell inexpensive rolls) with large lettering saying, "It's Your Special Day", "We Celebrate You," or another greeting.

- **Make a gigantic personalized "You Are Special" card** by stapling together two pieces of poster board and letting each member of the family make a drawing or poem for the card.

- **Prepare a special breakfast** of the child's favorites and serve it on a "celebration plate" (even a simple paper plate with a border of colorful stickers could be considered "special"). Use this plate to celebrate other special occasions during the year.

- **Light a candle by the celebrated child's place** at the table and decorate his/her chair with crepe paper.

Taking a little time to make a child feel uniquely special can be an invisible prize package of SELF-ESTEEM. Even in a large family or group gathering a particular date could be chosen, such as "Robert's Day" or "Kelly's Day," when the **celebrated child** would receive a surprise similar to any of the above suggestions. Ask the other children in the group for their suggestions on how to make their sibling, friend or fellow club member feel "special."

You Are Not Alone

Seek help on children's parties from experts: children, parents, and teachers who have successfully survived previous parties. **Ask parents** what ideas worked best; **ask children** which birthday was their favorite and why; **ask teachers** what group activities stood the test of time. Children four years and older literally "bubble" with ideas; your role may merely be to sift, sort, and direct their enthusiastic input into a party plan that includes elements like those listed in **GETTING YOUR FEET WET.**

Remember, you live with a resident expert on what makes parties tick: YOUR OWN CHILD. Ask for their opinions and suggestions. If your children are too young to offer an opinion, simply watch and take mental notes on what makes them happy. For example, center a party theme around their favorite activity, their favorite food or even their favorite time of day (See **TODDLER BREAKFAST BASH** or **MEANT TO BE MESSY** parties).

Don't be afraid to enlist the aid of indebted relatives, sympathetic fellow parents, unsuspecting singles, or even the neighborhood babysitter. There are more than enough positions available on the day of the party: ice cream server, cake cutter, photographer, clown, group leader, referee, etc. The larger your "**household staff**," the better chance you have of actively participating in the party and even enjoying the experience!

Be A Child Yourself

Step back in time and **approach the party with the same sense of fun as your child**. Let **SIMPLY CELEBRATING CHILDREN** trigger your own sense of fun and whimsy. It's your chance to create a magical situation where you are free to STOP and PLAY with your child without interruptions from the adult world. To set the stage, **ignite your imagination** with memories of favorite childhood songs, games or activities. Most importantly, try to **shape the theme of a party around your child's particular personality and interests**. If your child always requires the latest fad cartoon character as a party theme, then perhaps he has never been offered a more creative alternative. "**Being creative**" with a party can be as simple as doing what your child enjoys but with a **twist of theatrics** (see **Household Hocus-Pocus**).

Household Hocus-Pocus

There is an easy way to make magic for the children. Your stage of special effects can be **ordinary** household items presented in **extraordinary** ways. At least the kids will find your "theatrics" extraordinary simply because you've made the **usual** "unusual" for the party. Remember: It's easy to create this magic when you can **become a child again yourself** . . . if only for a few hours. Here's a sampling of quick change artistry around the house:

PROPS: Move furniture around to **create open spaces** or drape a sheet tent-style over clustered chairs with a broomstick as the center pole. This **creates a canopied area** for opening presents, eating refreshments, etc. Sitting on pillows or beach towels around an old tablecloth on the floor is unusual and fun to small children. Cardboard boxes make great tables and chairs for large groups!

For a quick air of festivity, **dangle colorful scarves** from lamp shades or doorways, **tie ribbon bows around favorite stuffed animals** and then "invite" the animals to attend a party (having these cuddly "friends" around is comforting to a shy child).

Cover a card table or child's gate with a colorful towel or blanket to serve as an impromptu theater. One great way to involve older children is to enlist their help as puppeteers to entertain the guests.

COSTUMES: A costumed SURPRISE GUEST of any kind will make magic happen at any party. The costumes don't have to be elaborate and the costumed talent can be quite amateur such as a neighbor, sibling, or even yourself dressed up as: a **clown** issuing balloons, a **gypsy** telling fortunes, a **magician** doing simple tricks, a dancing **Indian chief**, a friendly **ghost**, an old **witch** or aging **grandmother** to spin a tale, a **pirate king** or **fairy godmother** to lead a treasure hunt. Use your imagination by creating costumes from old sheets, baggy clothes, outdated formals and old jewelry. Simply change the tone and expression of your voice and the children will be spellbound.

If the appearance is brief and the anticipation of your party guests is high, a **SURPRISE GUEST** can add a special touch of excitement that will instantly turn an <u>ordinary</u> party into an <u>extraordinary</u> event.

Some young children might rather "**guess who's coming**" early and hear in advance what will happen when the "guest" arrives. This way they can anticipate who is coming without being overwhelmed by a sudden surprise.

Older children relish a <u>mystery</u>. To increase the suspense, leave clues to be solved about the "guest's" identity or tie the party's activities into a search involving the **SURPRISE GUEST** (see **Pirate Party** for details).

LIGHTING: Turn off the lights and **tell or read a story by candlelight** (the glow of candlelight can magically calm an active party and provide a quiet interlude). Or close the drapes and issue colored cellophane and flashlights (on short loan from the neighbors); the kids can **make their own light shows or shadow figures**. All you need is a blank wall and some background music as the backdrop.

SOUND EFFECTS: **Turn on a record or tape of lively music** to set a festive mood as the children arrive. Besides musical games, there are lots of children's participatory songs to get the party rolling or "take up the slack" if you have more time than activities (see the **ACTIVITY INDEX** for ideas).

Musical sounds can also be effectively produced by the children themselves. Use a tape recorder and take turns **recording each child's voice** telling a story, answering a question or singing. No matter what their age, children are fascinated by hearing their own voices.

Invitations Do More Than Invite

Every party really begins with the invitation so it's worth a little extra effort to make an unusual invite that accomplishes an important goal: **to create anticipation**, which can be half the fun of any party. If at all possible, have your child assist in creating the invitation. Even little children can lick the flaps on the envelopes and sign their names to the invite! Children also enjoy the excitement of delivering the invitations to all their friends.

Children love looking forward to special events. An invitation delivered one or two weeks prior to party time will ensure that your guests have not made other commitments. If someone was inadvertently left out or your child decides to add to the guest list (a parental nightmare), two weeks gives you time to make changes without hurting a child's feelings.

Wrapping It Up......................

No matter how carefully a party is packaged, there may be those trying moments which threaten to unravel your party plans. In order to **avoid some potential problems** you certainly didn't invite, try these simple strategies:

ORGANIZE many **fast** and **slow** paced activities (e.g., play several active games followed by a quieter one).

To help ease any competitiveness, announce that **EVERYONE** who participates in all the party games **will receive a special prize**.

Try to be **FLEXIBLE**. If one activity doesn't hold the children's interest, move on to the next. Have more ideas ready than you think you might need.

Divide large numbers of children into small groups and then **ROTATE** the groups to different "activity stations" so each child always has something to do.

To combat any "post-party blues," **SAVE** one family present to open last or invite one guest to stay an hour longer so the party won't seem to end so abruptly.

............................Some Final Thoughts

Panic-Free Party Check List

Steps To Follow:	Read For Ideas:
Plan a party that suits the interests of your children	**You Are Not Alone**, p. 4 **Be A Child Yourself**, p. 5
Send unique invitations	**Invitations Do More Than Invite,** p. 7 **Invitations** section of each chapter
Add magic with surprise guests, special effects & "mood maker" decorations	**Household Hocus-Pocus**, pp. 5-7 **Mood Makers** section of each chapter
Prepare fast, fun, & festive refreshments that reflect the "mood" of your party	**Refreshments** section of each chapter **Duckles Egg-stra Easy Eats & Treats,** p. 117
Select favor items that are durable, edible, or easily made by the guests	**Favors** section of each chapter **Duckles Egg-stra Easy Eats & Treats**, p. 117
Plan both quiet and lively activities that are suitable to your party location	**Activities** section of each chapter **Duckles Egg-Stra Easy Entertainment**, p. 111 **Activity Index**, p. 125
Ask adults <u>in</u> <u>advance</u> to help and then assign each helper a "special duty"	**You Are Not Alone**, p. 4-5
Be flexible, positive and prepared to have a good time with the children!	**Wrapping It Up**, p. 8 **Getting Your Feet Wet**, pp. 1-2

Duckles to the rescue.....

PARENT POTLUCK

Whether this party is a first birthday celebration or a lazy afternoon get together for friends and family, a **PARENTS POTLUCK** provides an opportunity for small children and their parents to meet and mingle playfully for a few hours. Invite your guests to **bring easy-to-fix edibles**. The party should be **low stress and low cost** so that everyone can simply relax, visit, play with their children and, of course, admire <u>your</u> newest addition!

Invitations

Type your announcement on a square piece of white typing paper and print copies to equal the number of guests. Each paper should then be folded into the shape of a diaper. Draw a diaper pin or place an actual safety pin on the front:

It's A Parent Potluck
To Celebrate Our First Year
With ________(name of child)
Bring finger foods and your family
COME STAY AND PLAY!
(Include date, time, place, etc.)

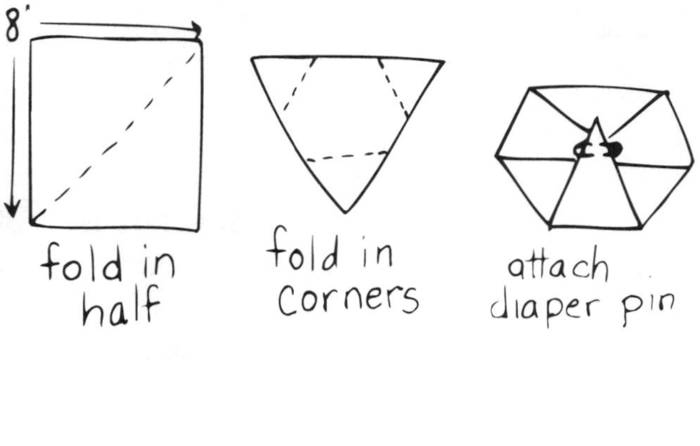

For an idea with a child's touch, have your child scribble any "design" on a piece of paper. Then write the following message in the remaining space:

Decoded Message:

Come To A Parent Potluck
To Celebrate Me
I'm One Now!!!
Bring finger foods and your family.
COME STAY AND PLAY!
(Include date, time, place, etc.)

Once you've printed the appropriate number of copies, deliver them in brightly colored envelopes with everyone's name scrawled in "kid's print."

MoodMakers

A unique and whimsical way to decorate is to recycle large, empty **diaper boxes** by filling each one with an arrangement of your children's toys or animals and add balloons for color. You can also tape the diaper box lids back in place, cut holes in the tops and **have fresh or dried flowers "sprouting" out of each box**.

One-year olds love having an abundance of **colorful balloons dangling from the ceiling on crepe paper streamers** (hang them low enough so kids can "bat" at them) . . . or **blow up inflatable beach balls** (borrow from neighbors if need be!) for children to toss into laundry baskets, boxes or open suitcases. Next, have everyone sit in a wide circle. Take turns calling out two children's names at a time. The two who are called must use their hands or feet to roll the ball back and forth to each other.

Refreshments

Try an ICE CREAM SMORGASBORD . . . **You supply the ice cream**. **Your guests bring toppings** such as flavored syrups, coconut, chocolate or butterscotch chips, cherries, nuts, marshmallows, etc. Scoop a variety of flavors into ice cream balls and freeze in advance. The guests can decide to place their creations in cones, paper cups or bowls (depending on the size appetite of each ice cream treat creator).

To satisfy all ages, have a POTLUCK OF FINGER FOOD. Should your guests need some ideas, here is a sampling of **"easy edibles"** to bring:

chopped raw vegetables
cheese cubes
sandwich meat roll ups
dried fruit

fresh fruit chunks
finger gelatin
raisins
assorted crackers

Each family would only need to bring one food item . . . all you need to supply are the drinks and napkins . . . it's easy for everyone to enjoy themselves!

Activities

> ***Please Note:*** All of these activities require parental supervision and, frequently, parent participation.

Sensational Sensations

Surround your toddlers with small-sized balloons, rolled-up "sock balls," or dry sponges in different shapes. Provide lots of different containers for filling, emptying or tossing practice such as suitcases, waste baskets, laundry baskets, clothes hampers, cardboard cartons, large plastic mixing bowls or buckets. **Parents can also "play" by filling and emptying objects** from one container to another . . . or helping children toss, catch and fetch the items.

For warm weather climates, fill an empty plastic swimming pool with a small amount of bubbly water (outdoors, of course!) and let the children kneel on towels to fill, pour and empty the "bubbly" with a variety of sieves, funnels, plastic containers, measuring cups and pitchers.

For cooler climates, place playdough or cornmeal in an empty plastic baby wash tub placed on the kitchen floor. Form playdough shapes with cookie cutters or scoop and empty the cornmeal into a variety of different-sized containers. Any extra cornmeal can easily be brushed off any surface.

Crawl-a-Thon

If possible, clear a large area of the room. Place all the babies at one end of the room with their parents stationed at the opposite end. The race is on! **Which baby can crawl or "toddle" the fastest** to rejoin their Mom or Dad? Parents can use their voices or wave a favorite toy if added incentives are necessary! Have an additional race where the parents crawl with their children to a finish line marked off with masking tape. This may be one of the few times adults can experience the world at "ground level" . . . just like their children do everyday!

Mattress Madness

Place a crib bed mattress on top of a twin bed mattress to create a **climbing and rolling area** (surround with pillows). The more mattresses or soft cushions the better, as toddlers love to take a soft tumble (limit this to only a few small children at a time).

It's A Wrap

Save odd scraps of wrapping paper all year and **wrap a large cardboard box** (the bigger the better). Since small children seem to love the unwrapping process as much as the present itself, they will love pulling off all the paper . . . especially if you have a few smaller boxes inside to unwrap before finding the **final surprise:** one last box filled with lots of small party favors.

Circle Classics

Holding their children in their laps, have parents sit close together to form a small circle. The old, familiar children's songs will never be "old" to the youngest generation. Have parents join their children for a songfest of such timeless favorites as: **I'm A Little Teapot**, **Mary Had A Little Lamb, Three Blind Mice**, **Twinkle, Twinkle Little Star**, **Old McDonald Had A Farm**, **Itsy Bitsy Spider**, etc.

Hang In There!

String up a clothesline (or two parallel clotheslines) and **drape them with sheets or scarves**. The bottom edges of the material should barely touch the floor. Children will love the sensation of running through the soft material. The clothesline could also be used to dangle scarves and suspend plastic buckets (or old purses) for filling and emptying with such objects as plastic poker chips, key chains, empty film containers, etc.

Parents Peep-Pie

Have someone take the children into another room. Then ask the parents to sit together on the floor and place a sheet over their heads. Call the children to return and ask them, **"Where did your Mom or Dad go?"**. After waiting a few seconds, all the parents should toss the sheet off their heads and shout, **"Peep-Pie!"**. Or ask each child to touch which head is their Mom or Dad under the sheet.

For another fun variation, **let the children place the sheet over their heads** and "surprise" their parents in the same way. Be prepared to repeat this activity several times because children never seem to tire of playing this timeless favorite.

Strike Out Swing Ball

Make your own ball by attaching a length of yarn to a paper grocery bag which has been stuffed with newspaper. Suspend the "bag ball" from a tree limb or any available door frame. Hang more than one "ball" if you have the space. **Hand each "toddler teammate" a rolled up newspaper bat and let each child take a swing**. The parents count out "1 - 2 - 3" swings before handing the paper "bat" to the next player. If you really feel energetic, **assign each player a "parent player**." Have the parent run with the toddler to different cushioned "pillow bases" once a child has had the chance to hit the ball one, two or three times (in this "game," the rules are very flexible!).

Walking The Plank

Locate a five or six foot long plywood board, approximately five or six inches wide and sanded smooth. Raise it to a slight angle by placing pillows or couch cushions underneath the board. Place a crib bed mattress or other foam pad where the ramp drops on one side. Have each parent hold their toddler's hand and guide him/her up the ramp. When the toddler reaches the top of the ramp, the parent can help him/her **make a "leap" and land on the bouncy mattress**.

Tunnel of Fun

Borrow folding tables from the neighbors and line them up in a row to form a tunnel, the longer the better. Cover the top and sides of the "tunnel" with sheets or blankets. The children will love **crawling through this mysterious maze**, especially if they are following parents who are "slithering" along on their stomachs ahead of them in the same tunnel!

Give each child a sealed plastic **bag of graham crackers or teething biscuits** and each adult a sealed plastic **bag of "wipes"** for future emergency uses . . . both tied with a brightly colored ribbon.

◦ OR ◦

As a different twist, **surprise the parents** with a parting gift: a **"time out certificate"** offering two or three hours of your time to baby-sit their children. Maybe your guests will return the favor someday! Use the example below or design your own "certificate."

Time Out Certificate

A party favor for PARENTS?

Yes!

Do yourselves a FAVOR !

Enjoy a gift of TIME - the chance to be alone for two or three hours while we watch your children.

Just give us 48 hours notice! We'll have fun with your kids while you kids" have fun!

Duckles to the rescue.....

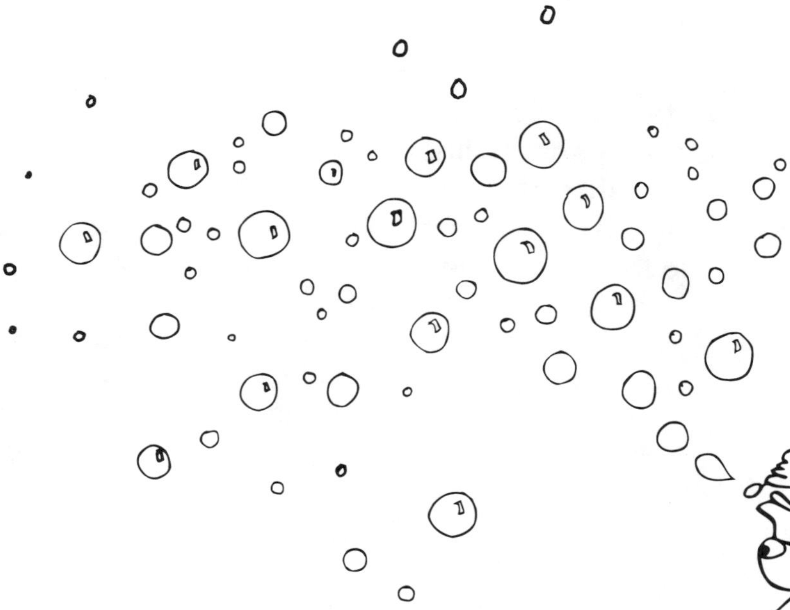

BUBBLES, BALLS, & BALLOONS

Since toddlers seem to travel in all directions simultaneously, this party offers "little busy bodies" lots of **action, color, and movement** to corral their energies. **B**UBBLES, **B**ALLS **&** **B**ALLOONS offers you the choice of one, two, or all three of the bouncing "**B**'s" in order to create instant magic.

Invitations

Cut white construction paper into a circular shape. Write your message in bright colors, then tape or staple a large enough piece of plastic wrap to the perimeter so it **looks like a puffy, clear bubble**. The message might read:

Write any invitation on **colorful paper balloon shapes**.
Glue a length of string to the base of the balloon.

◦ OR ◦

As a different twist, **let your favors become the invitation to your party**. For example, deliver a small rubber ball with a thin strip of paper wrapped around the ball which reads:

◦ OR ◦

Write this message on an **inflated balloon** with a permanent ink marking pen:

Mood Makers

Balloons everywhere! Dangle them from the ceiling on crepe paper streamers, attach them to lamp shades, walls or windows. **Tie a cluster of balloons to your mailbox or** tie them to little sticks so they line the walkway leading to your home. They also make excellent place cards. Simply attach one to every child's chair around the table and write the name of every guest on each balloon.

Refreshments

Carry on the party's theme by serving any of the following "round" refreshments:

Serve wrapped POPCORN BALLS or homemade CARAMEL CRUNCHY BALLS (see **DUCKLES EGG-STRA EASY EATS & TREATS**).

Prepare ICE CREAM BALLS and freeze ahead; simply serve with different toppings.

Create a BALLOON CAKE by frosting a two-layer cake with pastel-colored icing. Decorate the sides with colorful gum drops or flat, round mints as "**balloons**," attaching each balloon to a thin "**string**" of licorice.

Prepare a bundt or angel food cake, then place a BOUQUET OF BALLOONS in the center. Attach the balloons to reed sticks found in most party/paper goods stores. Hold the balloons in place by sticking the reeds in a mound of clay or a styrofoam base placed in the center of the cake.

Use a biscuit cutter to cut round shapes from sandwich bread. Tint cream cheese different colors with a few drops of food coloring. Spread each "round" with a color, then press thin licorice "strings" into each round to resemble the markings of a ball. You can make the "rounds" into BASEBALL, BASKETBALL, or SOCCER BALL SANDWICHES.

Activities

Musical Balloons

Play some lively music. The children must bat their balloons into the air as long as the music plays. As soon as the music stops they must **grab** their balloons and "**freeze**" until the music starts again. This activity can be repeated several times. Or, have the children **march** within a circle of chairs holding a balloon between their knees. When the music stops, they must quickly **sit down** on a chair without dropping their balloon.

Balloon Pop

Children divide into two teams. Two children at a time (one from each team) try to **sit on a balloon** and **pop it**. When it does pop, the next team member gets a try. The first team to finish wins. A **faster version** is to give a balloon to each team member, then see which team will be first to pop all of their balloons.

Balloon Relay

Place a large pile of balloons on one side of the room. Two teams of children must **carry the balloons** to the other side of the room holding them **between their knees** or **with their elbows**. The winning team is the one who can move the most balloons in the shortest time.

Balloon Ballet

Players divide into pairs and **link arms**, their free arms holding a round balloon between them. Once the signal is given, they must **keep the balloon up in the air** by "batting" at it as they "**dance**" their way to the finish line. If the balloon should drop, the players can stop and pick it up but they must **keep their arms linked at all times**.

Balloon-Buster

Tie a length of string to a balloon and attach it to each child's ankle. The players then try to pop as many of each other's balloons as possible **without having their own balloon popped** in the process.

Crazy Box Ball Drop

Save one or two large diaper boxes with front flaps that fold down. Spray paint the outside and decorate it to look like a crazy character or animal with the flap being its tongue, and the opening being its mouth. Use corks, bottle caps, foil, yarn, sponges, string, buttons, and other odds and ends to make hair, eyeballs, ears, a hat and nose. The kids will love **creating a "CRAZY CREATURE."** Its big mouth is the perfect place in which to throw ping pong balls, foil balls or sock balls. If you've made two characters, you can have a relay, letting each team member have one try to toss in the ball. The winning team is the one **tossing the most balls in the mouth**. Children may want to repeat this game and enjoy it even after the party is over!

Big Bubbles

To turn your backyard into a world of bubbles, pour **Bubble Brew** into several large, wide, pie tins (see **DUCKLES EGG-STRA EASY EATS & TREATS** for the recipe). Make **bubble blowers** by stretching a wire hanger into an oval-shaped hoop, then holding the curved handle, dip the hoop into the mixture and wave it through the air. Or, tape drinking straws together in a group, dip the ends in the "brew" and blow gently to create clusters of tiny bubbles. Even styrofoam drinking cups or the plastic peel-off rounds from a six pack can be dipped, blown through or waved in the air to produce **magical bubbles**.

Bubble Blow

Divide the group into two teams. Issue each team a pan of **"Bubble Brew"** and a tin can, opened at both ends (cover the ends with masking tape to prevent rough edges). One person from each team is to be the official **"bubble blower."** The "blower" dips the can into the solution and blows a bubble. Once blown into the air, team members must **blow or fan their bubble** (with a paper plate) to the finish line three yards away. If the bubble pops, they must return to the starting line for a new bubble. The object is to get the most bubbles over the finish line.

QUIET...

Bottle Bowling

Save your empty **plastic liter bottles**. Fill each one with a little sand or water to act as weights. Make a **clown face** (or any theme character) out of construction paper and yarn. Tape it on the front of 8 or 10 bottles. Give each child a ball and see **how many pins can be knocked down.** Keep score or just let each child throw two or three times.

QUIET...

Ping Pong Showdown

Place four empty plastic liter soda bottles along a ledge or table outside. Weight down the bottles by filling them with either sand or water. Remove the caps and place a ping pong ball on top of each bottle. Each child can then have a chance to **"shoot" the ping pong ball off each of the four bottles with the spray from a water pistol** (if available, household spray water bottles have a stronger spray and work best).

Should there be a large group of children, you might want to have several stations set up with four bottles in each. **Mark off a line for each child to stand on to shoot their pistol**. The distance children stand from the bottles should be based on the age and ability of your party guests. To draw out the length of the game, start with an easy distance away and then move the line a little further each time everyone has completed their turn.

QUIET...

Scoop 'N Blow Balls

Place a line of cotton (or ping pong) balls on the table. Have each child stand behind a cotton ball and see **who can be the first to blow their cotton ball across the width (or length) of the table**. For a large group, you might want to divide the kids into teams, giving each player a cotton or ping pong ball to blow.

Another variation would be to have each child sit on a spread out newspaper page. Hand each one a spoon and cup, blindfold them and place 10 to 15 cotton balls on the newspaper surrounding each player. When given the signal, **see who can be the first to scoop up all the cotton balls.**

Give everyone a small jar of **"Bubble Brew"** topped with a ribbon (see **DUCKLES' EGG-STRA EATS & TREATS** for the recipe) and have each child make their own **bundle of bubbles blower** by taping a cluster of drinking straws together. Just dip one end of the "bundle" in **"Bubble Brew"** and blow through the other end.

◦ OR ◦

Place a **STICKER** inside a balloon before you blow it up; that way, when the balloon <u>does</u> pop or deflate, the child will find a sticker inside. Issue these **"special sticker" balloons** as the children are leaving and whisper that there's a surprise inside.

◦ OR ◦

Make a one-of-a-kind **BALL OF FAVORS** by wrapping your own assortment of little items (gum balls, whistles, erasers, pennies, dice, etc.) with crepe paper until a small ball shape takes formation. Hand them out as the children are leaving so they can unravel their **"mystery ball"** at home.

Duckles to the rescue.....

TODDLER BREAKFAST BASH

Sometimes the most successful parties simply stem from everyday observations about the types of activities and interests that **make children the happiest**. The **TODDLER BREAKFAST BASH** is deliberately scheduled as a morning party to hopefully avoid any "pre-nap crankies" and begin a new day in a special way with a **sunrise** (or even late morning) **celebration!**

Invitations

Have your child color the perimeter of a plain, white paper plate with a yellow crayon. In the center of the "sun," write the following greeting:

RISE AND SHINE AT MY
BREAKFAST BASH!
Print date, place, time (as early as you wish)
COME AS YOU ARE . . .
JUST WEAR YOUR P.J.'S!!!!!!

Mood Makers

String a clothesline across the room and **hang up white lunch sacks** with clothespins. Use crayons to **draw different colored suns on each sack**. In the middle of every sun write the name of each child. As each child arrives, give him/her a **name tag with a colored sun** to match a sun on one

of the hanging sacks. Later, these sacks can be used to hold a variety of small, inexpensive favor items each child will receive for simply taking part in the games.

If possible, tie either regular or helium-filled balloons to the clothesline, **matching the color of every balloon with the colored sun on each sack**. Once the balloons are inflated, use a permanent marking pen to **draw a smiling face** on each one (a hint to start off the day with a smile?).

Since some of the children may still feel sleepy when they first arrive, **make the room "cozy"** with lots of pillows and blankets so they can snuggle or tumble, depending on their mood!

Refreshments

- Serve the birthday child's FAVORITE CEREAL or let the children choose from a variety of little cereal boxes.

- Offer sliced bananas, strawberries and raisins as "toppers" for the cereal or as added "morning munchies" for the party guests.

- Adventurous parents might want to offer toasted bread cut in quarters with toppings of soft margarine, jelly, honey and/or cinnamon sugar. Issue plastic knives and **let the kids do the spreading and sprinkling!**

- Offer several different juices or hand-out juice boxes.

- Spread out a blanket and have a "breakfast picnic" on the floor.

Instead of a **traditional** cake, make a DOUGHNUT LAYER CAKE by placing doughnuts on top of each other to create a "tiered" effect. The top doughnut would, of course, be adorned with candles for the birthday child. It's unique and easy to create!

TO HELP STIR THE SLEEPY PARENTS (who, incidentally, are <u>also</u> invited to wear their "P.J.'s" to the party), serve "face the day" coffee, tea, juices, croissants, sweet rolls or muffins.

Activities

Please Note: Ask parents to choose their toddler as a partner for all the activities.

Sheet Shake

Have everyone sit in a circle holding a bed sheet. Toss a number of bright colored balloons in the center. With everyone holding the edges of the sheet, **toss the balloons high in the air** and see where they land. The toddlers will probably want to repeat this several times.

Crazy Course

Parents and children follow a **twisting path of thick yarn or rope** laid on carpet or grass. The group can just walk along the yarn pathway or try these **"obstacles"** along the way:

- **rolling** a small ball down a cardboard wrapping paper tube
- **stepping** on and off of a small stool
- **jumping** across a mattress

- **running** through a sheet suspended on a clothesline
- **dropping** a clothespin into a bottle
- **tossing** a "sock" ball into a laundry basket

Hula Hoopla

Place four hula hoops in a wide circle with several feet between each one, leaving a clear, open area in the center (you may need to borrow a few hoops from the neighbors). Lay two of the hoops flat on the floor with the other two hoops held upright by the parents. When you play music, the children can **walk or hop around the floor hoops**, remembering to crawl through the upright hoops.

As soon as the music stops, each child must run to the empty center area and sit down. As soon as everyone sits down, the music can start again. If fewer children play, you can have them **run and sit inside a hula hoop circle** when the music stops. If possible, try to play different types of music. The children will enjoy dancing around with the hoops even after the game is finished, especially if you play some lively background music.

Oldies For The Young' Uns

Although some of the older children's songs may seem a bit "tired" to us, the youngest generation will find them to be fresh and exciting. Try Ring Around The Rosie with a new twist by substituting **hopping, skipping** or **tiptoeing** in the lyrics (for example, sing **Hop** Around The Rosie while **hopping** in a circle); also, sing London Bridge, I'm A Little Teapot, The Farmer In The Dell, Twinkle, Twinkle Little Star, Wheels On The Bus, Five Little Monkeys, etc.

Try to use motion and finger movements with the songs. Try creating a new variation of your own or ask children for their suggestions. Preschool and elementary school teachers are an excellent source of ideas. Also, your local librarian can suggest books and tapes with delightful songs for children.

Bucket Brigade

Collect or borrow four empty buckets. Fill two buckets with styrofoam packing pieces and leave the other two empty. Place the two full buckets on the opposite side of the room from the empty buckets. Divide the group into " teams of two's,"

each "team" consisting of a toddler coupled with his/her parent. To add a little excitement, gently **tie the leg of the parent to the leg of the toddler** with a scarf. Give both toddlers and their parents paper cups. Starting with full buckets, **see how fast the team members can carry cupfuls of styrofoam pieces from the full bucket to fill the empty bucket**. Anyone who participates is a winner.

"Feely" Fishing

Use a narrow piece of wood or broomstick handle to make an instant fishing rod. Hang a length of string from it and make a **"hook"** at the end using a pinch-type clothespin painted a bright color. Let the children take turns **dropping their fishing line behind the couch**. Hidden from view, an adult attaches a lunch sack to the "hook." After a child reels in the sack, he/she must first **feel** the contents and **guess** what's inside the sack <u>before</u> actually seeing their "catch." Also, individual items can be attached to the "hook."

The hanging clothesline **"sunshine sacks"**(see **MOODMAKERS**, page 28) can be used to hold each child's "catch of the day." Small, inexpensive trinkets, pennies, stickers, etc. should make excellent "fish" items since each child will want to go fishing quite a few times!

Suitcase Socks

Open up two or three large suitcases. Roll up lots of socks into balls (<u>clean</u> socks, hopefully!) and place them in a laundry basket. Tape off a line six to eight feet away and have the toddlers try to stand on the line and **toss their socks into one of the suitcases** (laundry hampers also work well and would be a bit more challenging). Have an adult standing by to keep the suitcase lids open and to toss socks back to the starting line.

Ramp Roll

To make an **instant race track for wheeled vehicles** inside the house, find books of similar size and lay them down side by side on the carpet to form a smooth surface . . . make as wide or winding a track as your supply of books will allow. Or lean a card table (with the legs folded) against a wall at a slant in order to create a "**raceway ramp**" for small toy cars.

"Bumper" Pillows

Ask each child to lay on their stomach on a pillow. Tie a piece of soft rope to one end of the pillowcase and have each parent pull their child slowly around the room while you play soothing background music. After a few minutes, switch to livelier music and **play a soft version of "bumper cars," replacing cars with "pillow autos."** The children will love "smooshing" into each other's autos, but gently!

Favors

Mark a circle with masking tape. Place little favors or pieces of wrapped candies within the circle. Let each child **toss several thin plastic bracelets into the ring, trying to land them around the favors**. You can also use plastic lids, with the center portion of the lid removed to leave a ring. Whatever favor the bracelet encircles can be taken as a favor.

Everyone has a chance to throw three to five rings into the circle and receive a limit of three to five favor items apiece. If a child doesn't succeed at circling a favor the first time, he/she can take another turn.

Finish the party with **favors children can enjoy making themselves**. One idea is to measure three strips of adding machine tape, about 2' long by 1" wide (if the children are old enough to use scissors, let them cut the paper strips themselves). Tape the strips to a tongue depressor stick, leaving a portion of the stick free to be the handle. Each child can color the strips with crayons, stickers or colored marking pens.

Once finished, these **SILLY STREAMERS** are fun to hold high and run with in the wind, swirl in the air, decorate the handlebars of a tricycle, or mark a favorite playhouse as a flag.

◦ OR ◦

Create another type of **SILLY WIND SOCK** by covering an empty toilet paper roll with a child's white sock decorated with glued sequins or buttons. The sock can also be covered with designs using marking pens or paint. Once decorated, staple strips of crepe paper to the edge of the cylinder. If you should want to hang the "wind sock," simple glue a popsicle stick across the open end of the cylinder and attach a strip of string or yarn.

◦ OR ◦

Another type of SILLY STREAMER can be made by cutting a Manila folder into a 3" wide strip. Help the children tape it together to form a circle. The kids can then tape different colored strips of crepe paper to the inside of the circle. Punch holes around the top and attach string to hang this from a tree, backyard play structure, or by the front door.

Duckles to the rescue.....

PRETEND-TO-BE

Here is the perfect party for SMALL children with LARGE imaginations. Although centered around dolls and dressing-up, any number of themes can be substituted: a **space** theme, a **toy truck** theme, an **animal** theme or a favorite **cartoon character**. **Let your child's interests be your guide**.

Invitations

Draw a lined border around the edges of a piece of typing paper to give the effect of a frame. Print at the top:

Find a Picture Of Who You'd Like To Be
Paste It Here And Bring It With You
To My
PRETEND PARTY!
(Write date, time, place, etc.)

- Younger children could be invited to **bring along their favorite doll or play figure** for more make-believe fun.

• Older children could come **dressed as someone they would like to BE** "when they grow up."

• When guests arrive with their pictures, let each child choose a **"new" name for themselves** . . . someone they'd like to be at the party. Have simple paper "name tags" ready so each person can wear their pretend name and be called by that name throughout the party.

Mood Makers

Suspend clotheslines around the room. Using clothespins, hang a variety of old **dresses, skirts, blouses, men's shirts, ties, scarves,** etc. Line up men's and women's **shoes, house slippers, boots, socks, hose,** etc. on the floor. Have a variety of **hats, purses and costume jewelry** available, even if it means borrowing a few items from fellow parents. **Wigs** and old **Halloween masks** can also add to the fun.

◦ ALSO ◦

Supply card tables, sheets and blankets so the children can **set up a pretend house, store, office, restaurant, hospital, or cave** at a moment's notice. Try to **provide a variety of household props** such as tablets of scratch paper, crayons, kitchen utensils (nothing sharp, of course!), pots and pans, plastic dishes, silverware, a children's doctor or nurse kit, gauze bandages, ace wrap, cotton balls, hair rollers, brushes, combs, empty shampoo bottles, wash cloths, diapers, baby bathtub . . . the list is endless! Also, any large, empty cardboard boxes (appliance boxes are ideal) can be adapted to help create **many different pretend play situations**.

Refreshments

At this party it's **not as important WHAT you serve as HOW you serve it.** No matter what your birthday child decides to choose for the refreshments, serve it with the added spice of **IMAGINATION**.

Help the children act out, step by step, how to follow a recipe and "pretend" bake a MAKE BELIEVE BIRTHDAY CAKE or a PRETEND PIZZA. Have lots of measuring spoons and cups, bowls, stirring spoons, rolling pins, plastic margarine tubs and empty spice tins to supply all the "pretend" sugar, flour, butter, spices, etc.

One of the final steps should be to place the PRETEND CAKE **or** PIZZA on a cookie sheet ready for the oven. As the final step you place it in the oven for a few minutes and then . . . PRESTO! . . . you pull out an **actual pizza** or **cake** to eat! (Of course you have prepared a pizza or cake in advance and placed it in the oven.) Ask each child to think of crazy names for their cake and punch when you serve the refreshments or you can offer a suggestion, (e.g.,**"Cinderella Kelly, your white snow cake and candy cane punch are ready now!"**).

◦ OR ◦

If the weather is nice, have the children **eat outside in one of the cardboard structures they constructed earlier**. The refreshments can be a part of their pretend play. For example, if the children have set up a hospital room, **serve the "patients" in their beds**, create a **tea party for dressed-up ladies,** or suggest warriors take time from battle to **feast in their fort**.

TO ADD MORE MAGIC . . .

Let the children sprinkle "magic dust" on their cupcakes or cake slices by giving each child a handful of colorful cake decorating "sprinkles." Some stores specializing in cake decorations even have a special "glitter" that truly gives cakes a magical sparkle.

Activities

Please Note: This birthday is much less structured than most parties so that the children will have more freedom to create and pretend.

Both you and your parent helpers should be available to help children put on "dress up" clothes (if they ask for help) or make occasional suggestions such as, "Maybe two of you could be the nurses and two of you could be the patients for a few minutes, then switch." Or suggest, "Would you like to have a visitor for dinner? I will be an old Grandma and come to your door in a few minutes for a visit." Invite parents to stay and "play" for 30 minutes.

The "visitor" can vary but **children seem to love adults occasionally playing a part in their make-believe world**.

Pretend Puppet Play

Drape a blanket over a clothesline or card table to serve as a curtain for the puppet play. Give each child a white or brown lunch sack or an old sock. Let them glue on bits of material, felt, sequins, styrofoam, corks, pipe cleaners, feathers, sponges, cottonballs, dried beans, macaroni, etc. . . . anything to make a "**crazy critter**."

What's the play to be about? Starting with the birthday child, let each child tell what his/her puppet is named and anything special it can do (the crazier the story the better). An adult can write the high points of each child's story and help them decide on a name for their puppet play. Assemble everyone behind the blanket in the order in which their puppet appears in the story. With a loud, expressive voice, one of the adults should read the story and let the children move their "**crazy critters**" to "**act out" the story**.

Make Believe Munchies

Yes! **EDIBLE PLAYDOUGH** does exist! Just consider all the possibilities! Children can **shape, roll, flatten, punch or form any number of pretend shapes,** decorate their shapes with raisins, coconut, vegetable sticks, red hots, peanuts, sunflower seeds, or chocolate chips . . . and then gobble up their own creations (see the recipe for **YUMMY GUMMY PLAYDOUGH** in **DUCKLES EGG-STRA EASY EATS & TREATS**).

Children's Charades

Here's a simple way for children to play this timeless favorite. Make up a list of possible **characters, situations or feelings** for the children to **pantomime** for each other (or the children may want to think of their own). Those in the audience try to guess what the child is trying to act out within a set length of time. Some children may feel more comfortable acting with a friend so you might prepare some suggestions that could be adapted for a "**partners charade**."

Suggestions for **CHILDREN'S CHARADES**:

(**CHARACTERS**) cowboy, doctor, pilot, bee, teacher, Superman, chef, librarian, fairy godmother, wicked witch, nurse, secretary, school principal, barber, hairdresser, old person, Indian, dinosaur, ostrich, lion, baby, construction worker, elephant, spider, etc.

(**SITUATIONS**) playing on a playground, watching a funny movie, riding a roller coaster, flying a kite, trying to catch a butterfly, going to the grocery store, putting together a puzzle, mixing up a batch of cookies, walking through a haunted house, playing baseball or soccer, performing gymnastics, flying an airplane, climbing a mountain, putting on make-up, eating bananas, etc.

(**FEELINGS**) frightened, happy, sad, angry, silly, nervous, tired, excited, disappointed, lonely, helpful, mean, strong, hurt, proud, embarrassed, frustrated, etc.

Shape A Work of Art

Group the children in teams of two. **Blindfold the team member who is to be the "artist" and tell the other children to choose a "pose"** such as crouching like a cat, standing with arms outstretched like a tree, sitting cross-legged like an Indian, or rolled up like a ball. You might help them by offering a few suggestions and then let their imaginations go!

The object is to find which blindfolded "artist" can be the first to **<u>feel</u> their teammate's pose and "sculpture" himself/herself into the very same pose**. This activity can't help but generate lots of giggles!

Pretend To Be Pantomime

This is a favorite activity for children because when using **"imagination magic,"** they can visit many "pretend places." Ask several adults in advance if they would lead the children in a pantomime at the party. Some possible places to visit are a trip to outer space, a haunted house, an amusement park, the wilds of Africa, etc.

One example would be, **"Let's go to the farm! Follow me!"** The children would then imitate the adult feeding the chickens, riding horses, milking cows, carrying buckets of milk to the farmhouse, churning butter, holding a baby duck, running from a squawking rooster, the more active movements you use with children, the better!

Most newspaper offices have rolls of newsprint in a variety of sizes at low prices. One roll supplies plenty of paper and is wide enough to allow children lots of space to draw a multitude of "pretend" pictures. Give each child a **small roll of** NEWSPRINT tied with a bow accompanied by a small BOX OF WATERCOLORS OR CRAYONS.

◦ OR ◦

Make up a large batch of PLAYFUL PLAYDOUGH (see **DUCKLES EGG-STRA EASY EATS AND TREATS**). Give each child a portion of the playdough in a sealed plastic bag tied with a bright ribbon. For extra fun, **include a cookie cutter** to make shapes with the playdough.

◦ OR ◦

Offer a quick and easy favor that's **EDIBLE!** Put a combination of any of the following "goodies" into a sandwich "baggie" for each child to take home: dried cereal, raisins, peanuts, coconut, chocolate chips, whole almonds, small crackers, dried fruit bits, or popcorn. Tie each baggie with a colorful ribbon or send home a larger amount for each child's family in a decorative tin can. **The kids can decorate the outside of the cans themselves with stickers, ribbon and colored paper**.

Duckles to the rescue.....

BRING YOUR OWN BEAR

Even an ordinary, loveable stuffed animal can become the guest of honor at a **BRING YOUR OWN BEAR** party. Since many children at this age are attending large group parties for the first time, guests are asked to bring along a favorite stuffed bear. Simply taking a familiar family friend to the party can offer the **"snugly security"** children need to try a new experience.

Invitations

Attach colored paper **ears, paws, tongue and bow tie** to a plain brown lunch bag. Use markers to add the **eyes** and **nose**. Then write your message on the sack:

I CAN'T BEAR TO HAVE YOU MISS MY PARTY!

Bring this sack puppet
with you
AND
Your Favorite Bear
(Place, Date, Time, etc.)

Mood Makers

Line up chairs back to back leaving an aisle down the middle. At the end of the chairs place a card table. Drape the chairs with sheets or blankets to **make a "tunnel" leading to a "card table cave."** When kids arrive, they can crawl down the tunnel and place their bears in the cave. You might even want to have the tunnel start at the front door and lead down the hallway.

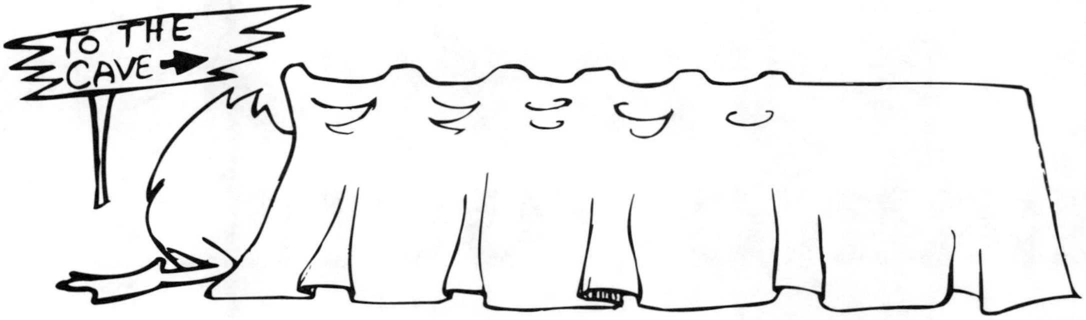

◦ OR ◦

Tie a helium-filled balloon to the arm of every child's bear and **place all the bears together in a circle as the centerpiece** on the table. Let each child make a **name tag necklace** for their bear. Write each bear's name on a piece of tagboard and let the children decorate their bear's name tag with crayons, bits of yarn, ribbon, sequins, etc. Punch a hole through the top and loop a piece of yarn through the hole to complete the necklace.

◦ OR ◦

Make a **Brown Bear Piñata** by stuffing a large brown grocery bag with styrofoam packing bits to act as filler. Make the same bear's face on the grocery bag that you used to decorate the party invitations.

Then add enough "goodie bags" so that each child will receive one once the piñata is broken. The "goodie bags" can be as simple as filling sandwich "baggies" with gum, raisins, pennies, etc., tied with a bow. Hang it up and let each child try several times to **hit the piñata** with a broomstick handle or bat.

Each child can easily become an **INSTANT BEAR CUB** by attaching two construction paper "ears" to the hair with bobby pins or attach the ears to a thin, plastic headband (see headbands worn by the ducks pictured below).

◦ OR ◦

Make **"Paw Prints"** by cutting circular shapes out of brown grocery bags and attaching black paper slivers as "claws." Leave a trail of "paws" on walls, doors and windows (see **BEAR PAW HUNT** in this chapter).

Refreshments

Make PAW-WICHES by cutting round shapes from bread (using a biscuit cutter), then spreading the "paw" with a mixture of honey and peanut butter. Press almond slivers or thinly-sliced licorice into the outside edge of each shape as "claws."

For another "beary" easy refreshment idea, try making **LITTLE BEAR CUPCAKES**. Simply frost a cupcake with chocolate icing, cut mints in half for ears, use brown M & M candies for eyes, a raisin for a nose and thinly-sliced licorice strips for the mouth.

Serve the cupcakes with BEARY PUNCH, a delicious mixture of fruit juice, sherbet, and soda that should satisfy every "growling" bear's thirst (see **DUCKLES EGG-STRA EASY EATS & TREATS**).

Activities

Bear Walk

Lay a winding pathway of thick yarn throughout the house and take the little bears on a walk through a "dark forest" to find a special treasure. As you tiptoe by different doorways, have the hidden adult let out a large **GROWL**. When that happens, **tell the bears they must hide in their cave** until you check to see that it's safe to travel again (this gives the "growling" adult a chance to move and hide in another room).

Time this so that the "treasure" they finally find is either the refreshments or the party favors. Children love the suspense of this activity and may become a bit "excitable" so plan to have a quiet activity afterward such as **THE BEAR IS AWAKE**.

The Bear Is Awake

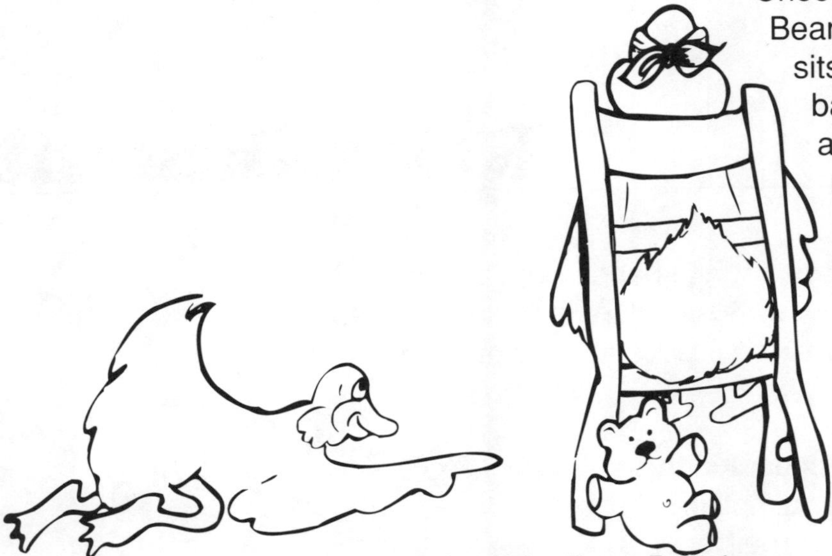

Choose one child to be the Papa Bear (or Mama Bear). That child sits blindfolded in a chair with his back to the group. A stuffed animal Baby Bear is then placed underneath the "bear's" chair. Everyone else sits in a semi-circle about six feet away. When you quietly whisper "GO," the first child you tap on the head begins to slowly **sneak forward to quietly kidnap the baby bear without "waking" the Papa Bear**. No sounds should be made. If the Papa Bear hears anything, he can swipe at the air around him, trying to tag someone without leaving his chair. If he touches someone, that person becomes the new Papa Bear.

"Bearable" Oldies

Although it may be "old hat" to you, reread **GOLDILOCKS AND THE THREE BEARS**, dividing the group into Papa, Mama, and Baby Bears with you or another child being Goldilocks. You can set the stage by having props such as a "porridge" bowl, a chair and a bed (actually a pillow covered with a baby blanket) so that the children, with their bear invitation sacks as puppets, can easily **act out this classic story**.

◦ ALSO ◦

Remember, as a child, sitting cross-legged in a circle of friends and chanting the words of **GOIN ' ON A BEAR HUNT**? Children of all ages enjoy acting out well-known stories or creating new ones they have written themselves. You might want to change a familiar story by adding locations in your own neighborhood.

Ask your children to sit in a circle and follow your actions. You can begin by rhythmically slapping your knees and saying, "Goin' on a bear hunt, goin' on the run, goin' on a bear hunt, goin' to have some fun" (or your group can go on a "duck hunt" or "snake hunt," etc.).

First we **open the door of our house (** *act out creaking open a door, then slamming it shut*), **slosh through the mud** (*cup your hands and make squishing noises*), **climb up a tree** (*claw the air upwards*), **look around** (*hold one hand flat against your brow and look right and left*), **climb down the tree** (*claw the air downwards*), **cross the lake** (*make swimming strokes*), then **come to a DARK cave**. We **s-l-o-w-l-y walk in** and (*growl loudly*) there's the bear!!! (*scream loudly*).

Hurry! Let's **run to the lake** (*slap your knees rapidly*), **cross the lake**, (*make quick swimming motions*) . . . etc. Retrace your route doing everything extremely fast until all of you return home and fall backwards on the couch or floor with a big sigh of relief (**WHEW!**).

Bear Toss

Here's a quick, simple activity that small children enjoy. Stretch out a sheet on the ground. Have the children place their stuffed bears in the center. Have everyone stand up and grab the edge of the sheet. After slowly counting to three, all arms should **lift the sheet into the air so that the bears are tossed everywhere**. Your party guests may want to repeat this a few times!

Bear Circle Tag

Place everyone in a circle with someone chosen as **IT** standing in the center. The players begin passing a stuffed animal bear around the circle. **IT must tag a child who is holding the bear** so everyone should pass the bear as quickly as possible from person to person. Once **IT** tags a child holding the bear, that child then becomes **IT**.

Another version would be to have the children sit up on their knees and quickly hand the bear from person to person **behind their backs**, **IT** still being in the center of the circle.

Running Bear Relays

Divide the children into two teams and **issue each "running bear" an old pillowcase**. Have the children step into the pillowcases and hold them at waist level.

With chalk or masking tape, mark a line approximately 20 feet from the starting line. On that line place a stuffed bear animal on a chair. At the signal, the first team member **must hop to the line, put the stuffed bear into the pillowcase**, hop back to the starting line, and transfer the bear to his teammate's pillowcase. The game is over when one of the teams has completed the relay.

Variation #1 of the Running Bear Relay:

To make the relay more challenging for older children, **provide only one pillowcase per team**. When a child returns to the starting line after having retrieved the stuffed bear, he/she must first step out of the pillowcase before handing it to a teammate. The teammate must then step into the pillowcase before the relay can continue.

Variation #2 of the Running Bear Relay:

Eliminate the pillowcases and **turn the relay into a three-legged race**. Using soft rope, tie the legs of two teammates together. Each team pair must then bring the stuffed bear back to the starting line **without using their hands**.

Variation #3 of the Running Bear Relay:

Follow the same relay rules as Variation #2 above except have each pair of teammates **run the relay backwards**!

"Bearfoot" Shoe Shuffle

Have the children remove their shoes and pile them in a corner of the room. Starting at the opposite end of the room, they must **run to the pile, find their own pair of shoes and put them on**. The first person to do this is the winner.

"Bearly" Moved Tray Test

Bring out a tray with ten items (for smaller children, display fewer items). Have the children study the tray for 30 seconds, then take away the tray and remove several items. **See which children can tell you what items disappeared**. For older children, remove the tray, then have them write down (or draw) as many items as they can remember that were on the tray.

"Bearly" Moving Room Test

Ask the children to carefully study everything in the room and try to remember what they see (allow 30 to 60 seconds). Then have everyone cover their eyes or lay on their stomachs with their heads down. While their eyes are covered, **remove an item from the room or change something to look different in the room** (i.e., reverse a couch cushion or remove a lamp shade). See who can tell what has disappeared or changed. To increase the challenge for older children, remove a very small ojbect from the room or slightly change the position of an item.

Favors

Have the children make their own BEAR BOOKMARKS by coloring narrow strips of tagboard and attaching a colored tassel of yarn at one end. A week or so before the party, have your child dictate his/her version of **GOLDILOCKS AND THE THREE BEARS.** After writing the story, have your child illustrate it, and then xerox copies. Give each of your guests the story rolled up in a scroll tied with a ribbon.

◦ OR ◦

As your guests leave, hand them the **BEAR BAGGIES** (the decorated bags they brought to the party). Ask each child to reach into the "**Bear Honey Pot**" (a basic cookie jar decorated with paper "bees") and choose two or three gift items such as **BEAR** cookie cutters, candies, magnets, pencils, stickers, stencils or other small items found in gift and toy stores.

Duckles to the rescue.....

MEANT TO BE MESSY

For this occasion, children **don't have to dress up** and parents **don't have to clean up** their home when the party's over because all the festivities take place **<u>outside</u>**. The **MEANT TO BE MESSY** party is the perfect solution for those adventurous parents who don't mind a short-term mess if it's for a good cause such as children having a TERRIFIC TIME!

Invitations

For an eye-catching invite, fill clear plastic sandwich bags with **handfuls of dirt.** Tie with a **bright ribbon** and **attach a big tag** that reads:

IT'S O.K. TO GET DIRTY
at my
MEANT TO BE MESSY PARTY!

Wear old clothes or a swimsuit
(List date, time, location, etc.)

Mood Makers

Tie balloons from the trees and **hang crepe paper streamers from the fence**. Attach a sign on the garage directing the children to go to the backyard. **Make your own colorful "wind socks"** by cutting an 8" wide, 24" long circular band out of stiff paper (file folders work well or paste sheets of typing paper together to form a wide cylinder shape). Tape colored crepe paper streamers to the inside of the band, punch holes in the top of the band and attach string. They can be hung anywhere for a festive touch. Children enjoy making these themselves.

◦ OR ◦

Hang assorted sponges from the branches of your backyard trees (simply poke a hole in the sponge and attach a length of string or fishing wire). Dangle them low enough so that **kids can bat at the sponges** with a baseball bat or an empty wrapping paper cardboard tube.

Refreshments

Fill a clean wheelbarrow with ice and cold drinks, frozen juice bars, juice boxes or homemade **YOGURT YUMMIES** (see **DUCKLES EGG-STRA EASY EATS & TREATS**) . . . whatever is cold!

For a snack that's fun to watch, as well as eat, try **SHEET SHAKE POPCORN**. Spread out a old sheet in the backyard and have everyone sit around the edges. Place a popcorn popper in the middle of the sheet (you will need an extension cord and remember that **this snack MUST <u>be</u> <u>done</u> <u>under</u> <u>adult</u> <u>supervision</u>!**). Keep the lid on the popcorn popper until the kernels begin popping. After the first few "pops," take off the lid and let the children watch. The **popcorn will pop out all over the sheet**. If the kernels land nearby, a child can reach out and **grab a bunch to munch!**

Save little plastic flower pots. Line each pot with foil, fill with ice cream and top with **crumbled chocolate wafers as the "dirt"** (if time is limited, use ice cream cups from the store). Cut colored paper into the shape of a small flower and write each child's name in the center. Paste the flower on the handle of each plastic spoon. Right before serving the FLOWER POT ICE CREAM, "plant" the flowered spoon in every pot!

The kids will go "buggy" over your **CATERPILLAR CAKE**. The caterpillar's body can be made of homemade muffins or cupcakes (peel off the paper wrappers before you place in position) or use prepackaged chocolate or pink snowball cupcakes. Simply arrange a string of cupcakes to look like a caterpillar "winding" its way down a table with lots of legs on each body segment and "bug" eyes peering out from below a set of antennae.

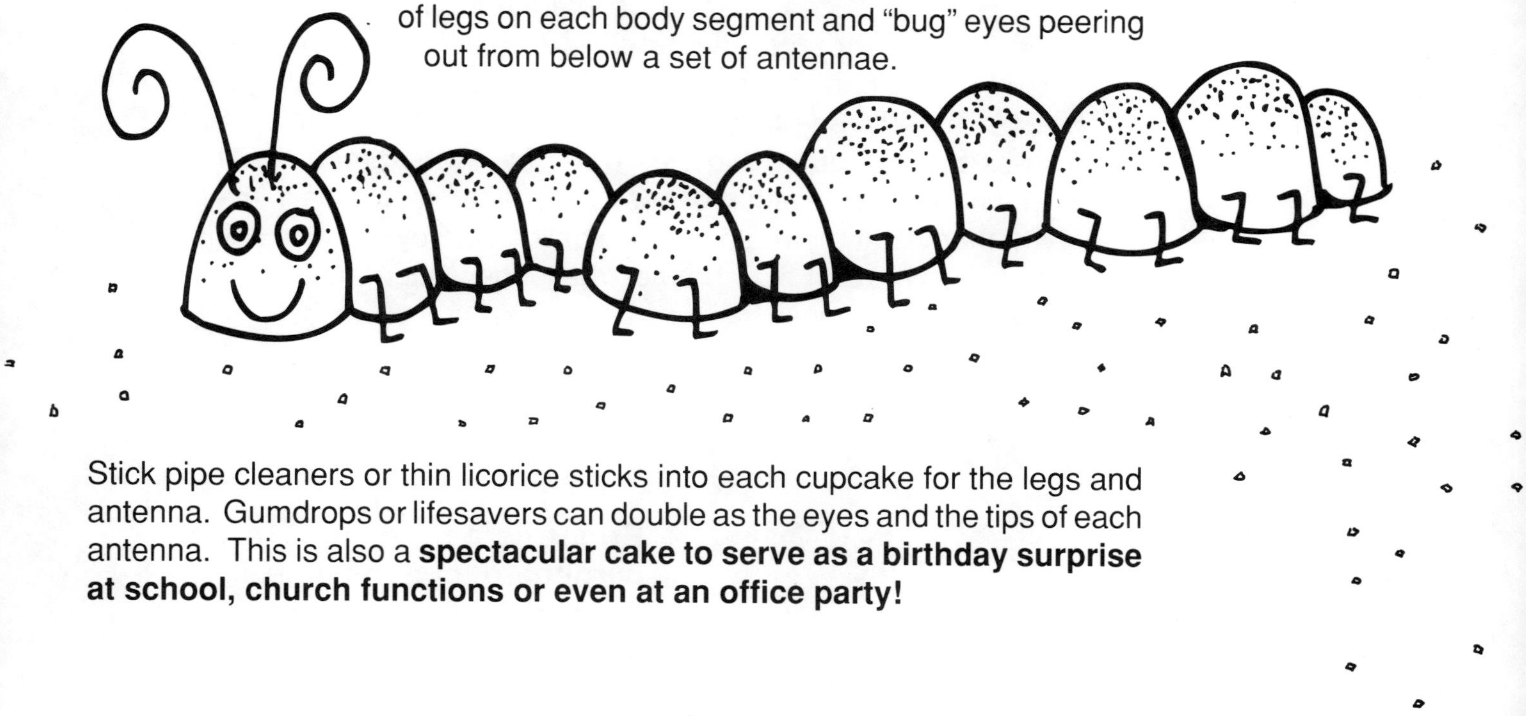

Stick pipe cleaners or thin licorice sticks into each cupcake for the legs and antenna. Gumdrops or lifesavers can double as the eyes and the tips of each antenna. This is also a **spectacular cake to serve as a birthday surprise at school, church functions or even at an office party!**

Activities

Tubs Of Fun

Choose two or three plastic tubs (or any old, odd containers) and place them outside. Fill them with **dirt, pebbles, sand, large rocks and water.** Provide an area such as a kiddie pool, plywood slab or a portion of cement patio to let the kids "**mix and mess**" to their heart's content. Any old mixing spoons, sieves, funnels, tin cans, paint brushes, buckets, watering cans, etc. will add to their pleasure.

Sheet Art

Hang up some OLD white sheets or butcher paper. Add a little powdered paint to the **BIG BUBBLE BREW** mixture (see **DUCKLES EGG-STRA EASY EATS & TREATS**). Using bubble blowers, let the kids blow lots of bubbles. When their bubbles pop against the sheet or paper, they will be amazed at the beautiful patterns that will be left behind.

Tail Tag

Each player places a rubber band around one of their ankles. Issue equal strips of crepe paper, asking that one end be tucked under the rubber band. When you give the signal, everyone runs around trying to **grab as many crepe paper "tails" as possible**, without losing their own "tail" in the process. The winner is the one with the most "tails" when the game is over. Another variation would be to tie balloons to everyone's ankle and see who can pop the most balloons without having their own balloon popped.

Box Of Art

Bring home several **large cardboard cartons** (the kind used to package refrigerators or furniture). Before the party, cut some irregular shaped holes in each of the boxes. Then **let the children leave their own mark** on each box using colored chalk and paint (follow **DUCKLES EGG-STRA EASY EATS & TREATS** paint recipe called **PAINT WITHOUT A TAINT** that usually washes out of clothes). In this case, anything goes . . . the artists can paint whatever they please on the big boxes or they might even feel "creative enough" to paint each other!

You might even join them!

Water Ball "Oon-ies"

Hand each player a **filled water balloon**. To start, have everyone pair off and face their partner only a few feet away. See if one child can **toss the balloon to the other without dropping it**. For every new throw, have everyone take one step backward so the distances become farther between players. The winners are the pair who can throw and catch the "water ball" the farthest distance without dropping it.

Water Cup Relay

All you need are four buckets (two filled with water, two empty) and a paper cup for every player. Each team must then **transfer water from the filled bucket** at one end of the line **to the empty bucket** at the far end. The first player must fill his/her cup, pour it into the next player's cup and pass it down the line until it can be poured into the empty bucket . . . **without spilling a drop!** If any water is spilled, the team must start over. The first team that successfully empties all the water from one bucket to another is the winner.

Nature Tag

Divide the party into two teams, reminding everyone to remember their place in line. Walk around the yard saying the names of different plants and trees. Then yell, **"Touch the maple tree!"** and everyone must **run, touch the tree and return to their EXACT position in line**.

Each time you name a different item. The winners are those team members who can return the fastest and remain in order. For older children, ask that team members touch two or more items before returning to their places in line.

Outdoor Scavenger Hunt

Before the party begins, go out in the backyard and find eight or ten **"nature" items** such as different shaped leaves, rocks, twigs, weeds, etc. Place them on a covered tray. Explain that once you uncover the tray, each child has 30 seconds to look at the items. When you give the sign they must **find as many of those same nature items as possible** in the backyard. Set a timer, giving younger children more time than older children to return. See who can find the most items from the tray.

Outdoor Obstacle Course

Set up your own obstacle course in the backyard with challenges such as: walking the path of a spiraling garden hose while carrying a full cup of water (not spilling a drop, of course!), climbing up and down a ladder while balancing a book on top of the head, jumping over a bucket, crawling under a picnic table, hopping backwards on one foot, shooting ping-pong balls off a plastic liter soda bottle with a water pistol, etc. You can **make it as easy or difficult as the ages of the children participating.** To add to the excitement, time the events and have the children cross a crepe paper "finish line."

"Chalkerboard" Toss

Choose a large area of a cement patio or sidewalk. Draw a special square for each child. Hand out colored chalk (toy stores have large sticks of special "sidewalk chalk"). Ask the children to **make a drawing inside the square** of something specific like a favorite animal, a rainbow, heart, or a spaceship design of their own choosing.

◦ OR ◦

Draw a large rectangular or shape on the sidewalk and divide it into squares. Write a different number in each square. Have everyone stand back six to eight feet. Give each child an even number of pennies, small stones, plastic lids, etc., and **see if they can toss the different objects into a numbered square**. The number in the square is the number of points the player receives for each object that lands in the square. The player with the highest number of points wins. For smaller children, follow the same rules **without keeping a tally of points**.

Let each guest "FIND A FAVOR." Wrap each favor in a different piece of wrapping paper (save your old scraps!). Hand each child a separate strip of wrapping paper. They must look in the backyard for the wrapped present that **matches their particular strip of paper**.

◦ OR ◦

Write each child's name in large capital letters on a piece of stiff cardboard approximately 4" x 12" in size. Have the children gather small twigs from the yard, then help them **glue the sticks in place, following the marked outline of each letter**. Once completed, punch holes at either end and attach a length of yarn, cord or string so that later these **PERSONALIZED NAMEPLATES** can be proudly hung on each child's bedroom door.

◦ OR ◦

Let each child PLANT SOME SEEDS IN A LITTLE FLOWER POT to take home (children can decorate the outside of the pot at the party if there is time). Also, some educational toy stores carry little magnifying **BUG BOXES** and pocket sized **MAGNIFYING GLASSES**, easy-to-carry necessities for every small outdoor explorer.

◦ OR ◦

Ask each child to wear or bring an old solid colored T-shirt (perhaps a white one "donated" by Mom or Dad). Buy several colors of fabric paint in squeezable tubes and let the children **PAINT THEIR OWN SHIRTS**.

◦ OR ◦

Make **HOMEMADE BIRD FEEDERS** by spreading large pine cones with peanut butter and then rolling them in bird seed. Attach a piece of yarn or string so that the children can hang them on a tree at home.

Duckles to the rescue.....

UNDER THE BIG TOP

Do you sometimes feel like your life is a circus? Well, now you can easily stage just such a circus in your own neighborhood! This unique party gives children a chance to actually "join" a circus and present their talent for the most receptive audience in the world: their own friends and family! So **send in the clowns** for a birthday party **UNDER THE BIG TOP**.

Invitations

Cut a colored paper triangle hat and paste it atop a round paper clown face. A smaller circle (or cotton puff) becomes the hat's pompon. Paste strips of colored yarn as hair, add crazy eyes, a red nose, wide mouth, big ears or a ruffle around the neck. Write the following message on the back of each crazy clown face:

COME CLOWN AROUND
AT MY PARTY
UNDER THE BIG TOP !!!!!

(Write your address, time, date, etc.)

You can ask all the kids to come as clowns or even wear their old Halloween costumes.

When the parents arrive with the children, have a poster (decorated with balloons) inviting the parents to come back in 1- 1/2 hours to see THE GREATEST SHOW ON EARTH. The birthday child can even issue the adults homemade tickets stating the time and place of the show and the admission price (free, of course!). Most of the party will be spent with the children planning a 15 minute show and/or midway to entertain the parents when they return (see the **ACTIVITIES** section for ideas).

Mood Makers

PARENTS! BE A CLOWN!!! It's easy to assemble a clown costume using old clothes (the more colorful and unmatched the better!), a crazy hat, big shoes, white face paint and bright red lipstick for cheeks and mouth. If you don't feel theatrical, ask a crazy friend or an older sibling to **"step into the spotlight."** As a clown you can have lots of fun with a dry, wide paintbrush to **"pretend paint"** the children's arms, backs, hands, etc. or simply attach 10 or more old scarves together (men's ties also work well) and tuck them into your pocket. The kids will love to **pull and pull and pull . . .**

If the circus is to be indoors, crisscross string or yarn from wall to wall in the smallest room and lay sheets on top of the webbing to give the effect of a "big top." Tape balloons from the **"sheet ceiling"** and from the walls. Set up chairs in a curved formation to look like **theater seating** and block off a portion of the room to be the **stage**.

If the circus is to be staged in an outdoor covered patio, **drape sheets or crepe paper from the patio cover**. If you have an outdoor party with no overhead covering, simply **drape crepe paper and balloons at the doorway** leading out to the circus area and hang lots of balloons from the trees.

◦ OR ◦

String colored strands of crepe paper from the center of the ceiling to the outer edges of the room for a **circus top effect**. Balloons can be effective mood makers if placed <u>anywhere</u> under the "big top."

Refreshments

CAROUSEL CAKE: Ice an angel food cake. Place peppermint sticks in vertical lines around the outside of the cake. Place plastic straws one inch apart as poles to hold the carousel "canopy" on <u>top</u> of the cake. To make the carousel canopy effect, attach a paper plate to the straws with dabs of icing. Glue little strips of crepe paper to the plate's rim and stick a toothpick flag on top (see the enlargement of the top portion of the cake). As the finishing touch, **position animal cracker figures in the icing** as a "parade of pairs" around the top layer of the cake.

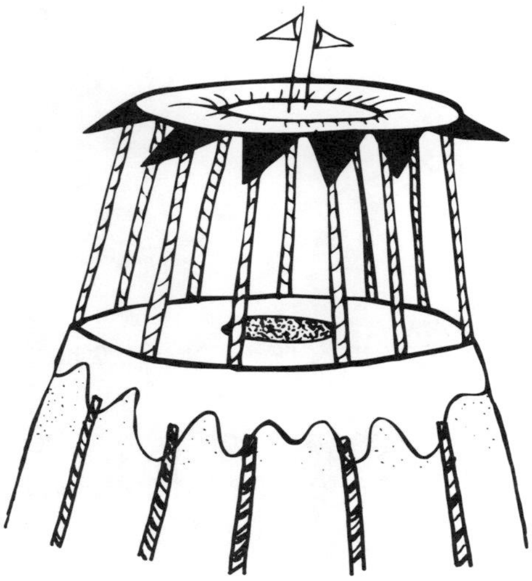

◦ OR ◦

If the party occurs during lunch or dinner, hang a poster board sign over the kitchen: "**REFRESHMENT STAND - HOT DOGS, POPCORN, SODA POP - BEST PRICES IN TOWN!**" Place popcorn in little bags, keep hot dogs and buns warm in a crock pot and serve sodas from an ice chest (Ginger Ale is be a good choice; if spilled, it should not stain the carpet!).

◦ OR ◦

CRAZY CLOWN CONES are fun to make as well as to eat. Scoop the ice cream into balls, make funny faces with red hots, raisins, licorice, chocolate chips, etc., then freeze in advance. Before serving, place a pointed sugar cone hat on top of each head. Children enjoy helping create the clown faces and will especially enjoy eating them!

Activities

Under The Big Top!

Ask the children to describe their **favorite circus acts**. Your job would be to list these acts and help the children find a way to perform them at THE GREATEST SHOW ON EARTH.

Everyone will need to use lots of imagination while enjoying the acts "under the big top" but that's the fun! Besides, with a **captive, clapping audience of enthusiastic parents, every act will certainly be a success**.

Here are some suggestions for circus performers.

Ringmaster: Dress the child in an old suit and make a cone-shaped megaphone out of paper so he/she can **announce all the circus acts**.

Wild Animal Act: Cut slits out of a cardboard box to **make a cage**. Then place several stuffed animals inside (or some of the children might want to **act like wild animals**). Tie yarn or rope loosely around their necks so the **"animal trainer"** can make them move at his command. He might want to carry rope as a pretend "whip" just in case one of the animals should escape.

Tightrope Walker: Place several bricks under a long 2" x 4" board (be certain there are enough bricks underneath to secure it and only raise it a slight amount). Then let your walker **"try" to make it across**. If you have a drum, add to the excitement by doing a drum roll at key moments.

You can also have children perform as **clowns**, **magicians**, **jugglers** or **fortune tellers** . . . even popcorn vendors!

Clown Face Relay

Cut out two identical sets of crazy clown face pieces such as eyes, nose, mouth, ears, hat, ruffle, etc. Place the pieces in two bags. When the relay begins, each team member must reach in the bag, pull out a piece and **stick it on a balloon "head" to create a clown face**. The winning team is the one who makes a face first **without popping the balloon**.

Circus Sounds Tag

Clear an open area with no obstacles. Blindfold one or even two children. The rest of the group moves around the area **making animal sounds**. The blindfolded children try to hear if someone is close by and tag them. Whoever is tagged becomes **IT** for the next game.

Make 'Em Laugh

Here's a quick, easy game for all the "clowns" you invited! Have everyone sit in a circle. Two children sit on chairs facing each other in the center. They each have **15 seconds to make the other person laugh** (tickling doesn't count!). The person who doesn't laugh gets to stay another round with a new "clown." If both kids laugh, then simply bring up two more "clowns" to take their places.

Another variation is to have everyone sit on chairs placed in a circle. The person playing "clown" does crazy movements and facial expressions to have as many people laughing as possible. As soon as someone laughs, they must turn their chair around so their back is facing the circle. **The last one left facing the "clown" in the circle will be the next "clown."**

Clown Around Carnival

Place three or four card tables around the room. Tape long strips of crepe paper around the edge of the table to form a "skirt." **Have a parent helper at each "booth" to supervise the activity**. Set up masking tape lines approximately four to six feet from two of the tables. Place the children in equal groups which can **rotate from one booth to another** (if necessary, set a timer to allow five or ten minutes per booth).

1) On one table place a small, medium and large mixing bowl (made of stainless steel or plastic). Have the children try to **toss five pennies into each of the bowls**.

2) Place five to ten glass or plastic soda bottles (weighted down with sand or water) on another table. Give the children plastic bracelets and see **how many rings they can toss over the necks of the bottles**.

3) Try a **face painting booth**. Simply find a set of bright colored watercolors and a small brush. Offer three choices such as a heart, star or rainbow and then paint their favorite picture on each child's cheek or forehead. Dip a damp brush into colored glitter and add **"sparkle"** to your final creation!

4) Play "hide a prize" by placing three paper cups on the table, turned upside down. Have each player cover his/her eyes while you place a prize under one of the cups (the "prize" could be any small favor item). Move the three cups around the table and then ask the player to guess **which cup is hiding the prize**. If the guess is correct, he/she wins the prize. If the guess is incorrect, the player may stand in line and try again.

5) Turn a cookie sheet upside down on a table. Tape a piece of paper to the cookie sheet **with the following pattern**: →

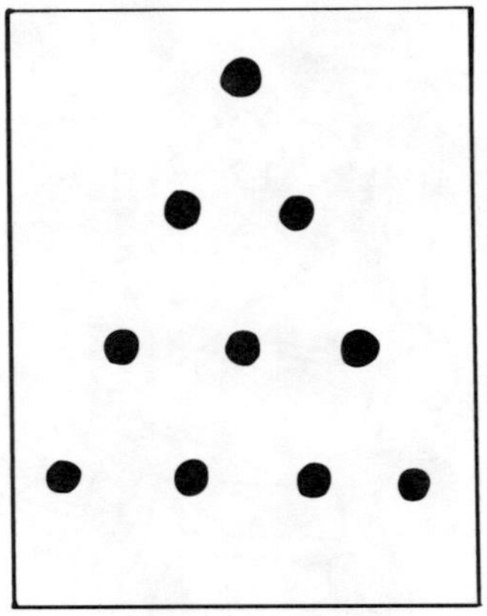

Place 10 dominoes on the pattern, one domino on each circle. In **"domino bowling,"** each player has three chances to knock down all 10 dominoes.

Hand out **bags of fresh peanuts** tied with a brightly colored ribbon and a **whistle on a string** (so every child can feel like a Ringmaster!).

◦ OR ◦

Issue special **"CIRCUS BALLOONS."** Place a clown or wild animal sticker inside a balloon. This way, each child will have a treat when the balloon deflates or pops.

◦ OR ◦

Try making "BIG Macs!" Simply fill balloons with dried macaronis (four or five in each) before adding air to each balloon. **Listen to the sounds and sights of the spinning macaronis** if the balloon is held up to the light.

> ***Please Note:*** Due to the small size of the macaronis, only use these balloons for <u>older</u> children's games that do not require the balloons to be popped.

◦ OR ◦

Tie a pencil on top of a box of **ANIMAL CRACKERS** with a **COLORFUL RIBBON BOW.** These decorated boxes can be placed in a circle or down the length of the table as a "circus train" centerpiece decoration.

Duckles to the rescue.....

PIRATE TREASURE HUNT

AHOY MATE! Take your birthday party on an adventure in search of hidden treasure. BEWARE **of Captain Hook!** He is <u>also</u> in search of the same treasure. **WHO will find it first?** Let a few simple "household theatrics" set the stage for an unforgettable **PIRATE TREASURE HUNT**.

Invitations

Cut an oval-shaped **"eye patch"** out of black paper, punch two holes on either side of the oval and attach two strips of yarn as the fasteners. <u>Since space is limited on the eye patch</u>, print this simple message in **silver or white ink**:

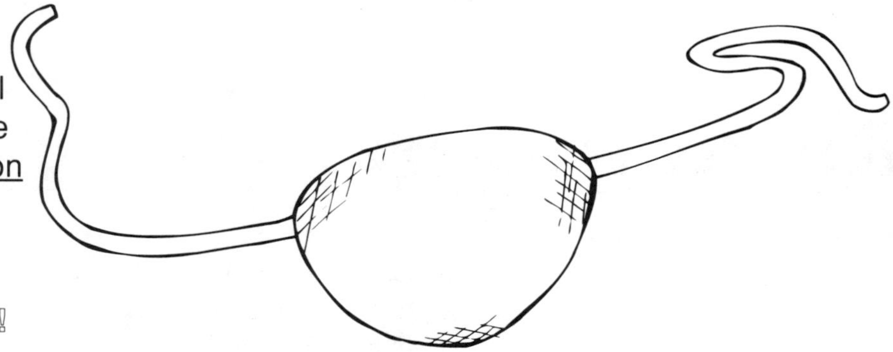

PIRATE TREASURE HUNT!
(Date, Time, Location, etc.)

When you deliver the invitation, ask each child to **wear the pirate patch to the party**. Some children may want to come to the party dressed as a pirate or a gypsy (see **MOOD MAKERS** for additional ideas on costume attire to wear for the "treasure hunt").

Mood Makers

Hang a **TREASURE MAP** on the front door to signify what adventures lie ahead. Make the map look "old" by crinkling or singeing a large piece of butcher paper. Then draw (or have your child draw) a simple map showing a winding path through mountains, around lakes, by palm trees, over boulders, etc. . . . ending up with a big **"X" where the treasure should be found**. Don't forget to add a pirate ship and/or skull and cross bones for effect. At the top of the map in large letters print, **"We must find the hidden treasure before Captain Hook. HURRY!** (draw a clock face) **Time is running out!"**

Dress as a pirate since your role will be to guide the other pirates to locate the treasure. It is an **easy costume to create**. Tie a scarf around your head, wear one earring, a wide belt, eye patch, and rolled up pants to the knees with either soft slippers or a pair of boots. A tall person with a low voice might dress as Captain Hook or at least be his voice during the party.

Tie **black and white balloons** together and attach them to paper cut-out shapes of **skull and cross bones.** Hang these shapes and balloons on any available lamp shades and/or walls.

Refreshments

No danger of a mutiny if you serve **CAPTAIN HOOK'S HOT DOGS.** Simply cut hot dogs into segments, then let the kids use "toothpick swords" to dip them in mustard and/or ketchup. Raw vegetables cut into large chunks can also be speared with "toothpick swords" and plunged into a creamy dip.

Pirates love **TREASURE SALAD**! Mix fruit cocktail with small-sized marshmallows and top it with coconut. Serve in scooped out orange or pineapple shells. Also, serve chips and powerful pirate **CANNONBALL PUNCH** (see **DUCKLES EGG-STRA EASY EATS & TREATS**).

For dessert, offer **CUPCAKE CLUES**. Make up a recipe of your child's favorite cupcakes. Before placing the cupcakes in the oven, drop a small rolled paper "scroll" in the batter of each cupcake with the final clue to the treasure written in permanent ink (see **TREASURE HUNT** for details).

Activities

Captain Hook By Candlelight

Have everyone sit in a circle, close the curtains, light a candle and begin **weaving your tale of the hidden treasure**. Speak in hushed tones of how . . . "many years ago, the entire area was completely underwater. It was at this time that pirate ships rode the high seas and Captain Hook was the meanest of all the pirates. Just a few days ago I was digging in the garden and **found an old scroll** (pull it out of your pocket). Listen very carefully. This is what was written on the old scroll . . . " (begin to read the scroll slowly, in a whisper):

*"The **ghost of Captain Hook** is still in search of buried treasure. The only way to rid the house of him is to do the following: Have a birthday pirate party on _________ (date of party), and join in all the party's activities. The treasure must be found before _______(the hour the party ends). **HURRY! Captain Hook is closer than ever to the treasure!"***

At this point your "stand in" **Captain Hook should release a loud, scornful laugh** from a hidden location. The kids will scream with excitement. The drama of the moment will inspire them to pursue the party's activities AND the hidden treasure.

Make A Map - Find A Treasure

Ask each child to silently choose a place in the backyard (or in the house) to **hide a treasure for <u>someone</u> <u>else</u> <u>to</u> <u>find</u>**.

Give everyone a blank sheet of paper and ask them to **make their <u>own</u> "treasure map."** Ask them to draw an "X" where the treasure is located as well as any landmarks that might help a fellow pirate locate the treasure more quickly. The "treasure" could be five or more pennies wrapped in foil or gold paper. Place the "gold coins" in each pirate's hand, advising them to hide the treasure quickly following their map's directions. Once everyone hides their treasure, they should exchange maps with a fellow pirate and begin searching for the **LOST GOLD**.

Walk The Plank

Elevate a long 2" x 6" piece of board a few inches above the ground. One at a time each pirate must **"walk the plank."**

Everyone must be careful <u>not</u> to fall overboard into the "ocean" below. If the children <u>do</u> begin to lose their step on the plank, create **the feel of instant ocean waves lapping at their heels** by spraying their ankles with water (the larger household spray water bottles work well). The pirates will love your "special effects," especially when you "command" them to do <u>more</u> than "walk the plank": ask them to **hop**, **walk backwards** or **sideways**, take **GIANT steps** or **baby steps**, **walk fast** or **very slow**, **close their eyes**, **crawl**, **walk on their heels** or **tip toe**.

While the children are having lunch, <u>remind</u> them that time is rapidly running out IF they are to find the treasure before Captain Hook does . . . **it's important for the "parent pirates" to keep up the suspense!**

Treasure Hunt

> ***Please Note:*** Start the **TREASURE HUNT** before serving dessert since the very final clue stating the location of the treasure will be baked into each child's cupcake.

Make enough clues so that each child can read one. Print each child's name on a separate clue and hide the clues before the party begins. Have a parent ready to help the children with any difficult words. The clues can rhyme, **"Look with care under the kitchen chair**," or be a simple drawing showing where the clue is located.

Let the birthday child begin the treasure hunt by reading the first clue. Following the clue's directions, the birthday child will then find the second clue. This clue will have the name of another child printed on it. Once found, the birthday child should hand the clue, unopened, to the person whose name appears on it. This avoids confusion and insures that every child will get a turn.

The very last child will read a clue that says, **"Eat your cupcake with lots of pleasure. Look inside for a clue to the hidden treasure."**

Important: **REMIND** the children that inside each cupcake is a paper clue and that **everyone must wait to read their clue at the same time.** You might need to remind the children to eat slowly as they will be anxious to finish their cupcakes and hear the final clue. Once **all the cupcakes are finished**, follow the instructions in "Dramatic Conclusion" on page 72.

Treasure Find!

Let a kitchen timer show that only a few minutes remain before they must find the treasure. At this point, your "stand in" Captain Hook should yell (from a hidden location), **"You'll never find the treasure before me!"** You then yell in return, **"Hurry kids! Let's read our final clue so we can find the treasure before Captain Hook does!"**

You then read aloud the final clue which should lead the children to the hidden treasure (see **FAVORS** section below). **Have Captain Hook appear and begin stalking towards the same location**, allowing the kids to get there first, of course! Depending on how dramatic an actor your Captain Hook is, he might stamp his foot, moan, groan, cry or otherwise show his frustration at not finding the treasure first.

The kids will love the victory!

Favors

As described in the **DRAMATIC CONCLUSION** above, Captain Hook and the children both head for the same location of the buried (or hidden) treasure. The treasure could be "buried" inside a jewelry chest or box hidden in a closet, under a couch or outside beneath a shrub.

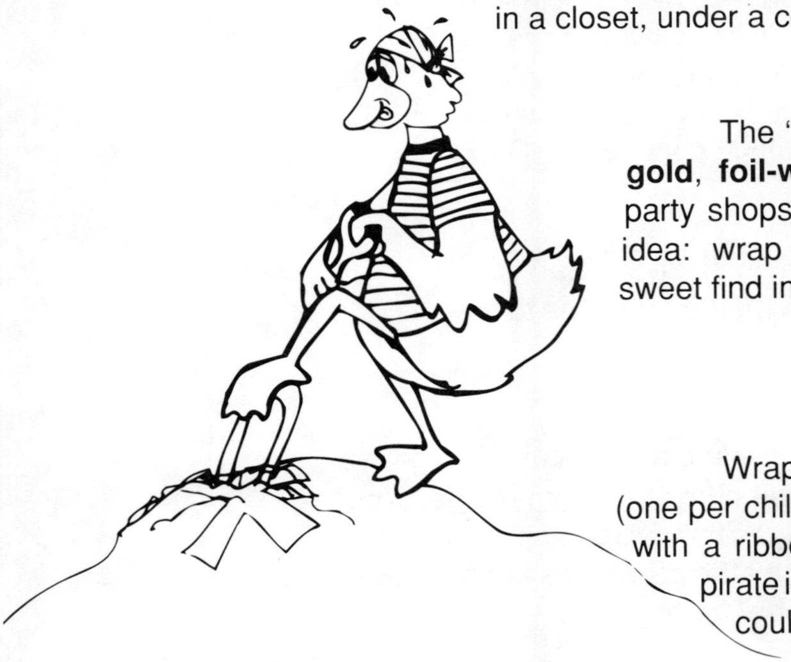

The "**pirate treasure**" could be a collection of **gold**, **foil-wrapped CHOCOLATE COINS** (found in party shops, import stores or candy shops). Another idea: wrap sugarless candies in cellophane or foil, a sweet find indeed!

◦ OR ◦

Wrap five to ten pennies tightly in a foil bundle (one per child) or **"bury" INDIVIDUAL SCROLLS** (tied with a ribbon), placing one ice cream certificate per pirate in each scroll. Any small wrapped party favor could be considered a treasure item!

◦ OR ◦

Assemble a **collection of small scrap lumber pieces and a tiny bottle of glue** (wood glue would be perfect for this project). Place the wood pieces and glue bottle in a bag tied with a ribbon to look festive and enclose this simple challenge written on a strip of paper:

AHOY MATES! GO HOME AND BUILD YOUR OWN PIRATE SHIP!

◦ OR ◦

You've heard of "sunken treasure?" This "treasure trough" is a **DIG FOR <u>HIDDEN</u> TREASURE!** Before the party, fill an old children's plastic swimming pool with sand, dirt, gravel, white styrofoam packing pieces, dried beans or even uncooked popcorn . . . then **bury lots of tiny penny toys as hidden treasure**. If you don't have a plastic pool available, use a large, heavy cardboard box, a wheelbarrow or even an dirt mound in the backyard.

Depending on the size of your "treasure trough," **allow two or more children at a time to dig for the treasure**. Little plastic play shovels work well as "diggers," or if not, give each child a small measuring cup or large serving spoon. Set a timer for 30 to 60 seconds so each child has the same length of time to dig.

Issue favor bags to hold any and all <u>discovered</u> <u>treasures</u>.

Duckles to the rescue.....

DINOSAUR DIG

STEP BACK IN TIME and **INVITE <u>DINOSAURS</u> TO YOUR NEXT PARTY!** Young children find these ancient creatures fascinating so why not include them in a special celebration? The children will delight in **hunting for ancient dinosaur bones**, **making their own "bag-a-saurus" to take home on a leash**, and all the other **prehistoric party pleasures** that will come to life at your **DINOSAUR DIG!**

Invitations

Cut colored paper in the **shape of a prehistoric animal** (many science shops and educational toy stores have stencils which are perfect for this purpose). Print this message on each shape:

COME HUNT FOR DINOSAUR BONES
AT MY PREHISTORIC PARTY!
(Write date, time, place, etc.)

If you have a <u>favorite</u> <u>dinosaur</u>, bring it along!

Mood Makers

Suspend pictures of different dinosaurs from the ceiling on pieces of string. If you are not an artist, use pictures from dinosaur coloring books (found in most educational toy stores). Ask arriving children to color the pictures, then find a **"hanging home"** for their dinosaur drawing. Attach a strip of crepe paper or adding machine tape to each picture and let each child choose where they would like to **"dangle" a dinosaur!**

Make the refreshment table look PREHISTORIC by grouping ferns and assorted green plants around a "watering hole" (a piece of cardboard painted blue). If possible, add some large river rocks for effect and place dinosaur figures in the scene. The children will enjoy moving their favorite dinosaurs around in this imaginary setting. If your party should be outdoors, place some large rocks in a sandbox or near a dirt pile to create a prehistoric setting.

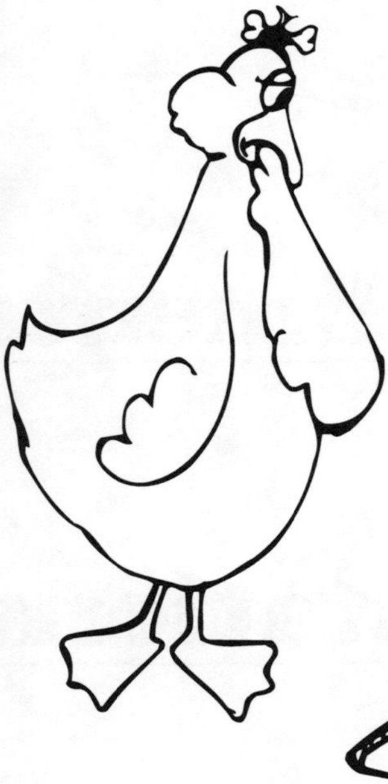

For more special effects, **cut out large dinosaur tracks** from brown grocery bags and place them on the walls and ceiling. These same tracks can be used for party games (see **DINOSAUR DOINS'** in the **ACTIVITIES** section).

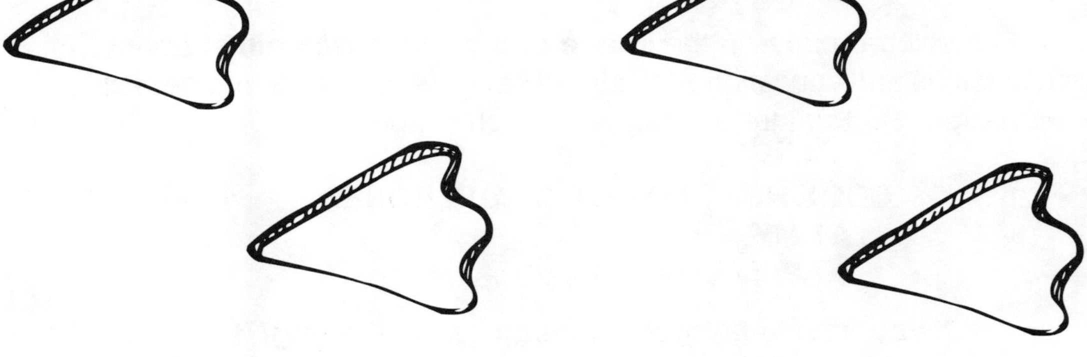

◦ ALSO ◦

As children arrive, help them get in a "dinosaur mood" by **creating their own dinosaur**. Hand out typing paper and have everyone draw a picture of their favorite dinosaur, then have each child hold up their picture and tell how they would care for their pet at home. Ask everyone to think of a name for their pet and let them **make a "pet dinosaur"** to **take home on a leash!** (see **BAG-O-SAURUS ON A LEASH** under **ACTIVITIES**).

◦ ALSO ◦

Have each guest **choose a name tag with a dinosaur sticker on it** (for a party of 12 children, there might be 4 name tags with pterodactyl stickers, 4 tags with stegosaurus stickers and 4 with tyrannosaurus stickers).

Once each child has chosen a particular sticker, write his/her name on the tag; this is an excellent way to group the children for activities during the party. As an example, you might say, "Will the **stegosaurus group** please go to the picnic table for a craft? The **pterodactyl group** can now hunt for dinosaur bones!" Name tags can be as simple as an index card with two holes punched at the top, looped with yarn to be worn around the neck.

Refreshments

Locate some **dinosaur cookie cutters** and make homemade cookies in different **DINOSAUR SHAPES**. Have raisins, chocolate chips, red hots, cherries, sprinkles, etc., available so that the children can add eyes and other features to give their cookie "personality."

For a lunchtime birthday, use the same cookie cutters to cut shapes from sandwich bread. **Let your little "dinosaur diggers" spread the bread** with peanut butter, cream cheese or butter and then decorate their shapes in the same way they would a cookie.

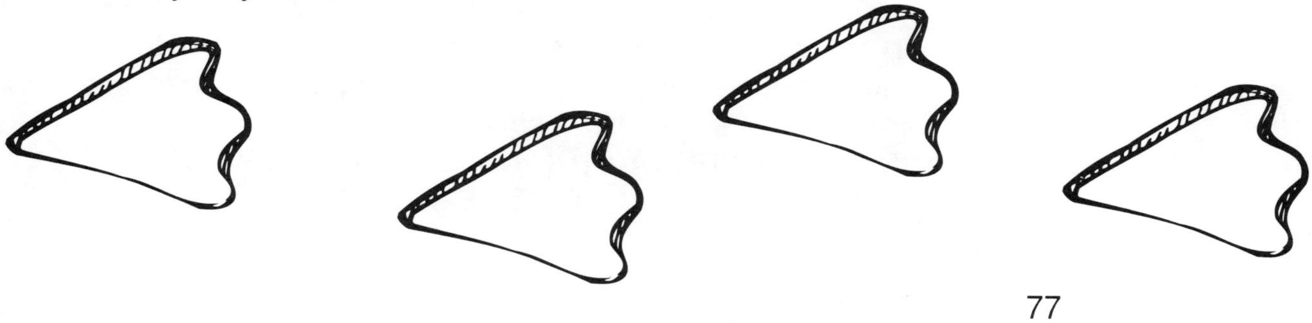

◦ OR ◦

Since **volcanos** were prevalent in prehistoric times, place two angel food cakes on top of each other. Squeeze the top cake slightly so both cakes form a **cone shape**. Drizzle melted red hots or pureed strawberries down the sides as **BURNING "LAVA" ON AN ACTIVE VOLCANO CAKE.**

◦ OR ◦

Make "refreshment favors" by serving **DINOSAUR DOUGHNUTS**. Buy a variety of doughnuts and place several little plastic dinosaur figures on top of each doughnut. Later, the little dinosaurs can be taken home as favors.

Amaze your dinosaur diggers with an erupting prehistoric party punch called **LIQUID LAVA**. Adding dry ice to your punch bowl causes the eruption (see **DUCKLES EGG-STRA EASY EATS & TREATS** for the recipe).

Activities

Dig For Dinosaurs, I

Ideally, this portion of the party should be outdoors. Before the guests arrive, **hide the "dinosaur bones."** These "bones" should actually be whitened chicken bones you have previously saved, washed in bleach water and dried in the sun . If your time is limited or the bones don't bleach out as white as you would like, simply dip them in a diluted mixture of powdered white tempera paint and water, then dry.

If your yard is carefully landscaped, you may wish to simply **lay the bones in various secluded spots** (similar to an Easter egg hunt). Should you have an available dirt pile and/or sand box, **bury the bones and issue each child a plastic shovel to dig for bones** (the shovels could also be their party favors to take home). Issue each child a sack to hold the bones for other activities (see **DINOSAUR DOINS'** and **DINOSAUR, WHERE'S YOUR BONE?** in the **ACTIVITIES** section).

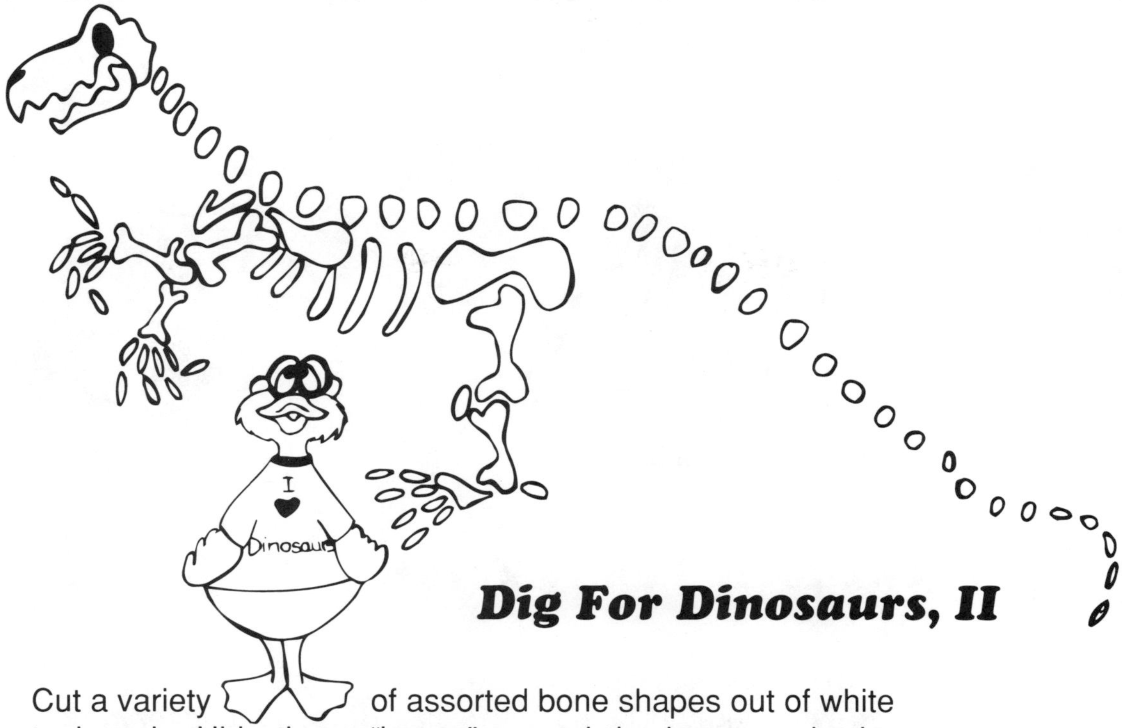

Dig For Dinosaurs, II

QUIET...

Cut a variety of assorted bone shapes out of white tagboard. Hide these "bones" around the house or in the backyard. Once the children have found all the "bones," **staple them together to form a giant dinosaur skeleton** to hang on the wall. **To add a little "theatrics" to the moment, weave a story for the children before they begin the "hunt":**

"Millions of years ago, gigantic dinosaurs roamed through this very neighborhood. *This very house was once a giant watering hole but one year it never rained and the watering hole dried up. As a result, many of the dinosaurs died from a lack of water. Their bones that still remain today are buried (or hidden) all around you. (Give each child a shovel and sack).* ***Good luck on your hunt. See how many dinosaur bones you can find buried in this yard****. Bring back any of your findings and we will look at the bones with a magnifying glass to decide which of the dinosaurs you have found."*

If possible, **borrow several magnifying glasses** so that each child can examine the bones more closely.

Bag-O-Saurus On A Leash

QUIET...

Trace the outlines of two dinosaur shapes on brown grocery sacks. Have the children color them with marking pens and cut out the shapes. Adults will need to help staple the two sides together, leaving room to stuff each shape with cottonballs or newspaper before the final staples are added. **Each child can choose a name for their pet "BAG-A-SAURUS,"** then attach the "name tag" on a yarn leash taped around their pet's neck. These "pets" make delightful favors to go home with each child.

QUIET...

Prehistoric Penny Toss

Cut out a large piece of cardboard and divide it into squares like an oversized checkerboard. Place a **dinosaur sticker in each square**. Place the checkerboard on the ground and tape off a line a few feet away where the players must stand and **toss their pennies**, trying to land as many pennies as possibly directly on the stickers in the squares. For older children, place the checkerboard on a table with a ladder placed a few feet away. They will love climbing **the ladder and tossing pennies onto the squares below**. To make the game more difficult, say the pennies must land on specific squares that you name or in certain formations such as a diagonal line, lines in the shape of a square or cross, etc.

QUIET...

Bread Dough Dinosaurs

Make up a recipe of your favorite bread dough or use a frozen prepared bread dough. Allow time for the frozen bread dough to thaw. Then let the children **create several dinosaur shapes with raisins for eyes**. Bake and serve warm with butter, honey and jelly or wrap them up for the kids to take home as "edible favors" to share (?) with their families.

QUIET...

Dream Up A Dinosaur

Provide a box of assorted odds and ends such as empty paper towel or toilet paper rolls, wire, ribbon, yarn, corks, paper clips, pipe cleaners, sponges, hair curlers, string, buttons, etc. Also, provide glue, scotch tape, masking tape and lots of popsicle sticks. Ask the kids to **make the craziest looking dinosaur in the world**. You'll love what they create and they'll love creating!

Caveman, Stir The Fire

Arrange chairs in a circle around an imaginary "campfire." The child chosen to be **the caveman or cavewoman pretends to stir the fire** with a large wooden spoon. The other children begin to walk around the chairs while chanting, **"Stir the fire! Stir the fire!"** When the "caveperson" decides to bang his/her spoon two times on the floor, everyone must scramble for a chair. The "caveperson" must drop the spoon and also find a chair. The child left without a chair then becomes "caveperson" and begins stirring the fire, thus starting another game.

Dinosaur, Where's Your Bone?

This simple but popular game begins with everyone sitting in a circle. Someone is chosen to be the "dinosaur" and is sent out of the room. Everyone puts their hands behind their backs and begins passing the bone from person to person while chanting, **"Dinosaur, dinosaur, where's your bone?"** The dinosaur "bone" can be a very small piece of cardboard shaped like a bone or an actual chicken bone.

When the "dinosaur" returns, he/she stands in the middle of the circle with a yardstick. When ready, the "dinosaur" gently taps someone on the head. When that happens, **everyone must stop passing the bone behind their backs and "freeze."** The person whose head was tapped must show their hands. If he/she has the bone, then he/she becomes the "dinosaur." If not, the "dinosaur" has two more turns to try to find the bone. After three tries, the "dinosaur" can choose someone else to be the next "dinosaur."

Balloon-A-Saurus Egg Hatch

Group the children into two teams and give each child a balloon. **Each balloon should be filled with air and contain one dinosaur sticker**. At the signal, a child from each team runs to a certain spot (marked with a masking tape "X") and tries to **"hatch"** (or pop) **their egg balloon by sitting on it**. Once their balloon "hatches," the child runs back to the team and the next child in line tries to do the same. When finished, each child will find a sticker inside their balloon so everyone wins!

Dinosaur Doins' (Assorted Games)

Use a large plastic Easter egg and if time allows, paint the egg an unusual color to serve as a **Dinosaur Egg**. Played like the traditional game of **Hot Potato**, the children sit in a circle. The egg is passed quickly from child to child as they pretend it is burning hot. A chosen leader sits in the middle of the circle with his/her eyes covered. When the leader decides to yell, "**STOP**" (or blow a whistle), the **child left holding the egg becomes IT** and gets to yell "**STOP**" in the next game.

◦ OR ◦

Have children try to **drop their "dinosaur bones" into a wide jar or bucket** while standing on a step ladder.

◦ OR ◦

Decorate a large-sized diaper box (the kind that has a flap in front) to look like a dinosaur, the flap being the tongue. Have the kids **"feed" the dinosaur** by throwing ping pong balls into his mouth (rolled up newspaper balls, sock balls, ping-pong balls or other items might be used).

You can also make an open-mouthed dinosaur with a shoe box, using the top lid as the fierce, menacing top jaw, edged with sharp teeth.

◦ OR ◦

Cut out ten or more large dinosaur tracks from brown grocery bags. Write a number on each track and place the tracks in a wide circle. If possible, play this game outdoors so you can tape the tracks to a cement patio or sidewalk. Have each child stand on one track. Begin playing music as the children begin to walk around the circle. **When the music stops, everyone must stand on a track**. You then draw from a jar of numbers and the child standing on that particular number wins a **PREHISTORIC PRIZE** such as a stick of gum, pencil or dinosaur sticker.

Favors

Right before the end of the party begin a **DINOSAUR EGG HUNT**. Have the children reach into a bag and choose a strip of colored paper. The color they choose is the color of the egg they must find (the small plastic colored eggs used at Easter). Inside each egg place a **tiny dinosaur or a dinosaur sticker**.

◦ ALSO ◦

Hand out whatever favor you choose in a MUSICAL way. Have everyone sit in a big circle. Play some music and begin passing the first wrapped favor from hand to hand. **The person holding the favor when the music stops gets to keep it (or open it)**. When the music begins again, hand the next favor around the circle. Repeat this until all the favors have been distributed. This is a great game to play if you need an extra activity to play at the end of a party.

◦ ALSO ◦

See **BAG-O-SAURUS ON A LEASH** under **ACTIVITIES** as a favor idea that children can make themselves and later take home.

Duckles to the rescue.....

PLAYGROUND PLAY-OFFS

Invite each child to be a champion . . . and what better location for a party than the wide open spaces of your **neighborhood playground?** Check with your local City Parks & Recreation Department (or school office if you're considering a school playground) for approval. With **adult supervision** and **careful party clean-up**, **PLAYGROUND PLAY-OFFS** can offer the freedom of movement only found in the out-of-doors.

Invitations

Have your child **draw a picture of a bike** with a black marking pen on a sheet of typing paper. Write this message, then photocopy the appropriate number of invitations:

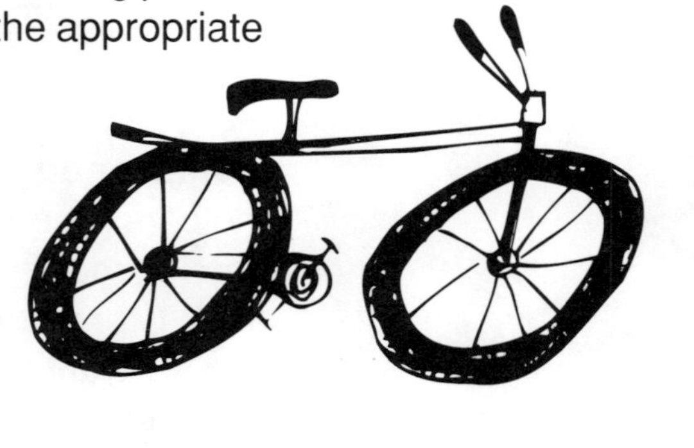

Draw yourself riding this BICYCLE
and HAVING FUN at my
BIRTHDAY PLAYGROUND PARTY!
(Address, date, time, etc.)

B.Y.O.B. Bring Your Own Bike!

Please Note: Does you child have a birthday during the winter months when bad weather may prevent the use of plagrounds? **Here's the solution! For an indoor location that allows freedom of movement, call dance, exercise or aerobic studios.** They may rent you the space and even provide a teacher to present a short class.

Mood Makers

Place a poster board sign near the entrance that says, **"ROBERT'S PLAYGROUND PARTY"** (or whoever is hosting the party). This will help direct children to the playground's entrance and will hopefully discourage any uninvited guests.

Hang lots of colored balloons and crepe paper from fences, picnic tables, swing sets or other playground equipment to add an **air of festivity**. If your school playground is a large area, you might tape or rope off boundaries and mark them with colored balloons to keep all the children corralled in one area.

Before the party begins, use chalk or masking tape to mark the start and finish lines of future relay games. If possible, make cardboard **START** and **FINISH** signs and tape them to sticks or yardsticks. Place the signs in empty coffee cans filled with sand and place them at either end of the relay lines. If you have an extra roll of crepe paper, stretch it across the finish line to make the event look even more official!

If you have invited a large number of children, **be sure that you have invited enough "helpers"** (one adult for every four children works well). The "helpers" might be encouraged to all wear the same color shirts and issue each person a whistle. In addition, it is a good idea to **bring a simple first aid kit** for small "boo-boo's" that might occur outdoors. The kit might contain non-sting antiseptic spray, several different sized bandages, antibiotic ointment, and a damp washcloth in a sealed sandwich bag.

Refreshments

Keep it simple with **two kinds of sandwiches** (e.g., peanut butter with jelly, tuna fish) and a big bowl of **CHIPS**. Depending on the season, serve **grapes, orange slices or watermelon pieces.** Since your birthday guests will most likely feel thirsty during the activities, be sure to bring a large thermos of water or punch for in-between events. **Juice boxes** are always a good choice to serve with a picnic lunch. Freeze the boxes in advance. By the time you serve lunch, the juice will be ice cold.

If your time is limited, **order a pizza** (some places might even deliver to the playground), **a bucket of fried chicken** or a **"party size" submarine sandwich**. These sandwiches usually come 6 feet long and you simply slice it into segments for your party guests.

Instead of a traditional cake, place candles on a CHOCOLATE CHIP PIZZA (make up a recipe of chocolate chip cookie dough, press it into a greased circular pizza pan and bake at 325 degrees for 25 - 30 minutes).

Activities

Please Note: Before any new activity begins, gather all the children and adult helpers together. Carefully explain the game rules, any particular safety rules and answer questions. For a very large group, plan to have two activities taking place at the same time.

Freeze & Thaw Tag

Someone is chosen to be **IT**. **IT** stands 10 to 15 yards away from the rest of the group who are to remain at the starting line. When the game begins, **IT** turns his/her back while the rest of the group begins to move forward. When **IT** decides to turn around, everyone must **FREEZE**. If anyone **THAWS** or moves, they must return to the starting position. The purpose is to be the first to touch **IT**. If someone gets close enough to touch **IT**, **IT** then turns around and chases everyone back to the starting line. Whoever is touched by **IT** at that time will be the next **IT**. This game can easily be repeated several times.

Bike Beauties

Let each child **"decorate" his/her bicycle** by winding crepe paper around the handlebars and wheel spokes. For an added **special sound effect**, attach a playing card to the rear fender of the bicycle using a pinch-type clothes pin. Any movement of the wheel will make crazy noises.

Bike Challenges

Mark off a start and a finish line approximately 8 to 10 yards apart. Have everyone pedal as hard as they can until they cross the finish line. Then everyone must **coast**. The winner is the one **who can <u>coast</u> the furthest.**

◦ OR ◦

Riding from the start to the finish line, see **who can balance the most magazines on his/her head** without toppling the stack.

◦ OR ◦

Discover **who can ride the SLOWEST** from start to finish without either foot leaving the pedal and touching the ground.

Air Antics

Issue sheets of 8" x 11" paper (a heavier bond paper works best) and let everyone try to **make a paper airplane**. For those who need help, a book entitled **THE PAPER AIRPLANE BOOK** by Seymour Simon has lots of wonderful ideas for airborne creations. Also, you can staple paper plates together (either back to back or front to front) to form **saucer shapes that fly**.

Let everyone begin at the same starting line you taped off for the bicycle races (see **BIKE CHALLENGES** in this chapter). The object is to toss the flying creations into the air as many times as necessary until they are "flown" across the finish line. These flying creations can also be decorated with marking pens and taken home as favors.

Crazy Cans Relay

Divide the party into two teams. Then divide each team in half, placing each half facing each other about four to six yards apart. **Give the first person in each line two 1 lb. coffee cans**. Given the starting signal, the first team members from each team place one can down, step up onto it with both feet, set the next can a few feet away, step onto it with both feet, grab the other can and place it down, step onto it, etc.

Each player must "walk" on cans until they reach the next team member who must then "walk" the cans back to the other side. To successfully complete the relay, every team member must **complete a "walk" on cans from one side to the other**.

Obstacle Drop

Make two identical obstacle courses positioning milk cartons or wastebaskets so that the **bikers must ride through an "S" pathway**. Tie yarn or string between the handlebars of each bike so that the children can hang approximately eight pinch-type clothespins on the yarn or string. As they ride through the course, they must **drop one clothespin into each container**.

A challenge for older children would be to drop their clothespins into <u>smaller</u> containers such as 1 lb. coffee cans.

"Winner" Olympics

Here is an **"Olympics"** where **EVERYONE CAN BE A WINNER.**

Events could be as simple as hopping, skipping, or running races; measuring how far each child can either throw a ball or jump from a standing position; how many times within a minute each child can **jump rope**, **hit a ball** into the air with a racquet (using ping-pong or tennis balls) or **kick a ball** through a series of markers (coffee cans or plastic liter bottles mark the course).

◦ OR ◦

Try a combination of crazy events. One event might require entrants to run backwards through an obstacle course while **A)** balancing an aluminum pie plate on their head; **B)** holding a balloon between their knees; **C)** balancing an egg on a spoon; **D)** blowing through a straw to keep a feather floating upwards in the air; **E)** hopping on one leg like a flamingo, crawling like a spider, squat-hopping like a frog, waddling like a duck, wiggling on the ground like a snake.

Each child who enters an "Olympics" event receives a **painted washer "medal"** that can be worn on a string necklace. Spray-paint these washers a variety of bright colors as the children will enjoy collecting their "medals" just for participating in the games. When parents come for their children, invite them to be the audience for a special **AWARDS CEREMONY**.

Chain Reaction Tag

One person is chosen to be **IT**. Whoever is touched by **IT** must hold hands with **IT**. Slowly **IT** acquires a **long chain of people to help IT touch and tag other people** to add to the chain. Only the persons at each end of the chain can tag other people. The last person to be added to the chain becomes **IT** and begins the next game. This is an excellent first game "icebreaker" activity.

Stuck On You Tag

One person is chosen to be **IT**. Wherever **IT** touches someone is the place where they must **"glue" their hand** (not moving it) while they continue to keep away from **IT**. If **IT** ever manages to touch a person's feet, they must sit down and are out of the game. The more people get **"stuck on themselves"** the easier it becomes for **IT** to touch their feet. The last person still able to move around can either be **IT** in the next game or can choose someone else to be **IT**.

Cement Shoes Tag

Mark off an 18' x 24' rectangle with chalk. Someone is chosen **IT** and stands in the middle while the rest stand together at the narrow end of the rectangle. When a signal is given, everyone runs from one end of the rectangle to the other while **IT** tries to tag as many people as possible. **Those tagged must stand perfectly still, their shoes "cemented" to the ground**.

A second signal is given and everyone runs back to the opposite end. This time anyone who is "cemented" becomes **IT** and can tag other players, but **cannot move from where they are standing**. Anyone tagged becomes "cemented" and becomes another **IT**. The game continues until there is only one person left to run through a "mine field" of "cemented children."

Favors

Give each child one of the balloons used to decorate the playground plus a small **BICYCLE LICENSE PLATE** personalized with the name of each guest (many drugstores and gift shops sell these items). Other possible **"outdoor items"** for use as favors would be water pistols, frisbees, sun visors, jacks, jump ropes and little "bouncy balls" (these items can be purchased fairly inexpensively at toy and party specialty stores).

◦ OR ◦

An appropriate gift would be a <u>small</u> roll of reflective tape that the children could place on their bicycles for extra safety when riding in traffic. Place the tape in a plastic bag along with some bike "**SPOKE BEADS**." Most toy and bicycle shops sell these beads. They snap-on the spokes, look colorful and make sounds when the wheel turns.

Duckles to the rescue.....

DO-IT-YOURSELF

Here's the solution for parents who don't have much time but do have a strong desire for a **unique party**. A **DO-IT-YOURSELF PARTY** allows children to **pitch in** and **help themselves** to a good time while you **bow out!**

Invitations

Fold a blank sheet of typing paper in half lengthwise, leaving the front of the invitation blank. Inside have your child print (then make photocopies):

HI _____ (name of guest),
You're Invited To A

DO-IT-YOURSELF PARTY!

(Write date, time, place, etc.)

DECORATE THIS INVITATION YOURSELF
And Bring It To The Party.
You'll Win A **PRIZE!!!!!**

Also, bring an idea for a game to play!

Mood Makers

When guests arrive, have the children tape their decorated invitations to a wall or door for a colorful effect. Specify which room(s) are to be decorated, then issue crepe paper (adding machine tape can also be used for streamers), old bows, balloons, ribbon, streamers, confetti, etc., and **let the children "go to work" decorating rooms for a party**.

Another idea would be to stretch a long roll of blank paper along a wall or window (most newspaper offices sell rolls of inexpensive newsprint). Using crayons, magic markers and chalk, let each child add their artwork to a special **"make-it-yourself mural**."

Supply plain white styrofoam cups, napkins and plates. White sheets of typing paper (taped together on one side, then flipped over) can easily become "placemats." Provide colored marking pens, crayons, and a stamp pad set or stickers so that **each child can easily personalize and decorate their own party paper goods**.

Refreshments

Let your party guests create their own **ICE CREAM or CUPCAKE CONCOCTIONS**. Serve plain cupcakes and/or scoops of different flavored ice cream and let the children add the toppings. Place individual bowls of cherries, chocolate sauce, whipped cream, coconut, little marshmallows, sprinkles, red hots, chopped nuts, sliced bananas, granola, chocolate chips, strawberries . . . the possibilities are endless! **Let the children vote on who has the most "creative" concoction** and award that person the "golden scoop" (a plastic ice cream scoop painted gold).

◦ ALSO ◦

Your **do-it-yourselfer's** will love making their own **MUNCH MIX**. Just place sandwich baggies by bowls of crunchy dry cereal, popcorn, pretzel sticks, peanuts, chocolate chips, raisins, dried fruit bits, etc., and let everyone create their own snack.

◦ OR ◦

Another fun idea is to mix a batch of **COOKIE PARTY PAINT** (see **DUCKLES EGG-STRA EASY EATS & TREATS**) and let the kids brush colorful designs on cookie shapes. No time to bake? Use packaged graham crackers or vanilla wafers.

Activities

> ***Please Note:*** Since the children were "invited" to bring game ideas (**INVITATIONS**, page 93), allow enough time for each child to name a favorite game to play. If many different games are suggested, party guests could form groups and **rotate from one game to another** so that the children play a variety of different games.

Statue Wraps

Gather the children into small groups of three or four persons. Hand each group a roll of toilet paper and instruct them to choose one child as the "statue." Explain that each group has exactly ten minutes to **wrap their "statue" from head to foot** using the entire roll of toilet paper. No further suggestions should be given so that the children can discover their <u>own</u> method of wrapping the "statue." The first group to finish wins.

Another variation would be to issue a roll of toilet paper to the group and see which group can create the **most imaginative fashion, costume, or character** using the entire roll of paper.

QUIET...

Back-To-Back

Hand out blank typing paper and have everyone **draw their favorite THING** (an animal, food, place, person, toy, etc.). Mix the pictures up and **pin one to each person's back**. Everyone must then **ask each other questions** about what is on his/her own back. The questions are limited to one per person and must be answered by **YES** or **NO**. Once a person guesses what picture is on his/her own back, they sit down. If a child has asked every person one question and still hasn't guessed their own picture, he/she may then ask someone a second question. This is a good "**icebreaker**" **activity** to begin a party.

QUIET...

Name A Game

Divide the guests into several different groups and ask each group to **make up an original game**. Provide objects that could be used in a "homemade game" such as a deck of cards, cardboard squares, circular milk carton lids, dice, balloons, shoe boxes, ping pong balls, etc. Give prizes to the group that comes up with the **most unique idea** (it could be a tie so plan to have enough prizes for every player!).

LIVELY!

Sack Skits

Before the party, have your child take three sacks and place five or six unrelated items in each one. These items could be as different as a brush, hammer, tissue paper, envelope, scarf and a stick of gum. At the party, divide the children into groups and give each group a sack. Ask them to **think of a story they could act out** using each one of the items. It's amazing what skits their imaginations will create!

Draw & Guess

Hang up a large piece of blank paper. Hand the first child a large marking pen and ask him/her to think of something to draw. Without saying what it is, ask a child to only draw a few lines of what he or she is silently thinking . . . then stop and sit down. The next child should look at the lines, think of **what it might be** and **add a few more lines** to the drawing.

This continues around the group **until there is a finished picture** (it's fun to have each "artist" tell what picture he/she had in mind to draw). If the picture is completed before everyone has had a chance to draw, just ask the next person to start a new drawing.

Picture Perfect

Divide the party into two teams and give each team a stack of ten blank cards. Have the team members **write the name of one person, place, or thing** on each card (without the other team hearing their choices). Hang up a large sheet of blank paper. The teams exchange cards and then, alternating words, each team member has one minute to **DRAW** what is written on the card while the other team members **try to guess what is being drawn**. There can be no verbal clues. Everything must be drawn. The winning team will be the ones who correctly identify the most drawings.

Another Twist

Divide the party into teams. One person is chosen to be the "artist" and stands before a large, blank piece of paper. The rest of the team is given a simple picture such as a big square, oval, heart, etc. (The "artist" should NOT be allowed to see the picture). You then give the signal and **each team tries to tell their "artist" what to draw without saying the exact name of the object to be drawn**. For example, to draw a square the artist might be told, "Put a dot at the top left-hand side of the paper. Now draw a straight line from the dot to the right until we say **STOP**. Now draw a straight line going downwards, etc."

Mystery Motions

Everyone sits in a large circle. One **child is chosen to be the "detective"** and must leave the room. While the detective is gone, a leader is chosen and everyone in the circle must follow what the leader does (clapping hands, touching noses, pulling ears, shaking heads, nodding, hunching shoulders, snapping fingers, etc.). The group should **try to follow the leader** without looking directly at the leader since the object of the game is to **confuse the detective**.

When the detective returns, he/she has 15 seconds to identify exactly **who is leading the group**. Everyone can have a chance to be the "detective" by rotating turns around the circle.

Make Up A Silly Story

Place 8 sheets of blank paper in front of you. Write a different heading at the top of each such as **favorite colors** (two per person), **favorite place, favorite food, favorite number, favorite animal, least favorite activity, most favorite activity, favorite cartoon character** (two per person).

Go around the room and list everyone's responses under each heading. **Make up a "silly story"** leaving blanks throughout for you to fill in with the information given by your party guests.

For example, "Once upon a time there was a funny girl (or boy) named ________ (**fill in with someone's name at the party**). She had (**fill in favorite number**) ________ eyes and (**favorite color**) ________ hair. More than anything in the world she wanted to build a (**favorite place**) _________ next to her house because she had nothing to do all day but eat tons of (**least favorite food**) ______________. She had a (**favorite color**) __________ best friend who looked like a (**favorite animal**) __________. Sometimes her Mom and Dad acted like (**favorite cartoon characters**)__________. More than anything in the world she liked to (**least favorite activity**) _________ all day long. If she was very, very good her parents would let her (**most favorite activity**)_____________ for six days without stopping.

A story framework could be written in advance on any subject or simply leave blanks throughout a familiar bedtime story, then "rewrite" it using the children's responses.

Pretend To Be Pantomime

Prior to the party, look through a stack of old magazines and **cut out pictures that depict activities** (an exercise class, fishing on a lake, painting a house), animals, cartoon characters, occupations (a doctor, teacher, football player, etc.), or even common indoor and outdoor items (a couch, lamp, tree, lightning, sun, etc.). Paste the pictures on individual pieces of construction paper, allowing one or two pictures per child.

Divide the children into two teams. Place the stack of pictures face down on a chair about eight feet from the two teams. At the signal, one player from each team must run to the pictures, grab the top one, privately look at it and then **pantomime what is shown in the picture** (using only silent actions and gestures). The first team to guess all the pictures, wins.

Favors

Glue four tongue depressor sticks together to **form a star pattern**. Paint or color them, then glue on seeds, beans or glitter to make a **HANGING DECORATION** for their room (also lots of fun to **throw as a Frisbee!**).

◦ OR ◦

Mix up a batch of **ARTSY ART DOUGH** that can be modeled into beads, animals, faces, monsters, dolls, etc. (see **DUCKLES EGG-STRA EASY EATS & TREATS**). The dough shapes could be taken home on wax paper and should harden overnight. Have several colors of mixed paint available. Let each child choose one color and send it home in an empty baby food jar, perhaps with a small, inexpensive paintbrush.

◦ OR ◦

Let the children create their own **PERSONALIZED FAVOR** to take home. Choose one type of inexpensive, solid-colored plastic item such as a mug, pencil or knickknack box, visor, large comb, headband, flashlight, ruler or even switchplate cover! Provide colored permanent marking pens or decorative, adhesive stickers and watch each child **decorate an item with their own individual style**.

Duckles to the rescue.....

BANANAS BACKWARDS

This celebration offers a **different twist to the usual party routine**. Since older children have attended quite a few parties over the years . . . this particular occasion offers experienced party-goers the chance to literally turn the tables and invite their guests to go **BANANAS BACKWARDS!**

Invitations

Fold a sheet of paper in half **lengthwise** and write this message on the very "**back**," keeping the rest of the invitation **blank**.

YOU'RE INVITED TO A
CRAZY BACKWARDS PARTY!

WEAR YOUR CLOTHES BACKWARDS
AND COME TO THE BACKYARD.

IF YOU WANT TO BRING A GIFT,
PLEASE BRING IT UNWRAPPED!

Tell your invited guests to **hold their invitation up to a mirror for the translation**:

YOU'RE INVITED TO A
CRAZY BACKWARDS PARTY!

WEAR YOUR CLOTHES BACKWARDS
AND COME TO THE BACKYARD.

IF YOU WANT TO BRING A GIFT,
PLEASE BRING IT UNWRAPPED!

Mood Makers

At most parties, the presents are opened near the end of the party. Since this party is "bananas backwards," the guests arrive with **unwrapped packages**, hand their present to the birthday child, he/she says **"you thank"** and then proceeds to immediately **WRAP** it . . . definitely **backwards manners**! Be sure to have lots of used newspaper (or wrapping paper), bows and tape available for the "backwards birthday child" to easily wrap the gifts after having received them!

Post a sign in the front yard (written backwards, of course) inviting all guests to go to the **backyard** and enter through the **back door**. Greet guests by saying "**GOOD-BYE**," give favors immediately (see **FAVORS**, page 109) and have everyone walk backwards once they enter inside. Give each guest a **NUTTY NAME** name tag with their name written backwards and ask that everyone call each other by these names throughout the party.

A quick method to make your decorations appear especially "crazy" is to use old party remnants. For example, hang used Christmas ornaments on an indoor plant, place some colored plastic Easter eggs on the table, string some Valentine's Day hearts across a doorway, tape a Halloween witch to the front door, the more "mish-mash" of items, the better. Turn both the refreshment table and chairs **upside down** and wind crepe paper around the legs, hang **deflated balloons**, and have a record playing at too slow or too fast a speed as appropriate **"background"** music.

Refreshments

Remember to **change the sequence of events** so that you eat the refreshments and cake **first,** then sing any "celebration song" such as a **backwards version** of the "Happy Birthday" song ("You To Birthday Happy!"), blow, and then finally light the candles. The candles can be placed in what remains of the cake or in a decorative holder.

Make **INSIDE OUT SANDWICHES** by placing two pieces of sandwich meat on either side of a single piece of bread. Or place the bottom half of a hamburger bun between two thin hamburger patties.

Here's another idea: serve **DAFFY DRINKS & DIZZY DIP**. Have everyone drink from juice or soda cans turned upside down. Use a bottle opener to punch a hole in the can, then use a straw to sip the drink. **DIZZY DIP** can be any dip served with chips. To be "backwards," first lick the dip off the chip, then eat the chip (or serve crackers or vegetable sticks).

For the perfect "backwards" birthday cake, how about a **PINEAPPLE UPSIDE DOWN CAKE** or cupcakes turned **upside down** with a little icing on the bottom? For an easy "backwards" treat, make **CRAZY CONES** by serving scoops of ice cream with the cones placed on top.

Activities

Don't Follow The Leader

The **backwards version** of this timeless favorite is that a "leader" is indeed chosen, but **everyone does the opposite** of whatever he/she commands them to do. If the "leader" says to "stand still," you can "hop" or do anything else **except** "stand still." This game encourages children to concentrate, especially since the rules of traditional games are completely "backwards."

To make the game of **RED LIGHT, GREEN LIGHT** backwards, if the leader says "Green Light," the line must **STOP** (instead of moving forward as is usually done). In turn, when the leader says "Red Light," everyone can be free to **MOVE FORWARD** (instead of coming to a stop as is the usual rule of the game).

Strange Stories

Pick a book of well-known fairy tales or nursery rhymes. Begin at the end and **read the story or poem backwards** or **read the last line of a familiar bedtime story**. See who in the group can name the title first.

◦ OR ◦

Write simple one sentence endings to a story, one for each child. With the children seated in a circle, read an ending, then let each child have the chance to **make up a quick story that would fit the ending.** Then ask each child to **say their favorite animal, color, food, singing group, etc.** <u>**backwards**</u> (e.g., pizza would be "azzip"). Try to "translate" what each child says.

Memory Madness

Sit everyone down and give them five minutes to **"memorize" everything they see in the room**. Then have them leave the room while another adult reads them a story appropriate to the party's theme such as **INSIDE, OUTSIDE, UPSIDE DOWN** by Stan & Jan Berenstain.

This "story time" gives <u>you</u> a chance to **"remodel"** the room. Choose items like a lamp, sofa pillow, wastebasket or chair to turn upside down (or modify in some way) as well as smaller items such as a magazine, book, telephone, place mat, etc. For example, close a book that was open, wrap the phone cord around the telephone, or flip a place mat to the reverse side.

When the kids return, give them five minutes to **silently count** all the **"topsy-turvy" items** they can locate. Each child sits down when they have a total and of course no one reveals their number. The winners are those who have located the correct number of items.

Bottoms Down Volley-Balloon

Divide the party into two teams and issue each team member a chair. Arrange the chairs so that each team is sitting down in two rows facing the other team. Place a length of string as a divider "net" between the two groups and mark off rough "out-of-bounds" lines with masking tape. The game is played following general volleyball rules with the exception of two "backwards" changes: **all team members must remain with bottoms down on their chairs at all times** and a large-sized balloon is used instead of a ball. This is a terrific game for any group gathering, especially with adults playing their children.

Silly Soccer

If the children are familiar with the game of soccer, it is fun to play a backwards version where the children must **run backwards and kick the ball with their heels** instead of the side or toe of their foot. Or have someone be the "crazy referee." Whenever the "ref" blows the whistle, everyone must freeze in place until the whistle is blown again. A variety of sports can be switched into reverse, backwards play . . . older children will enjoy making up new, crazy rules for the game.

Mixed Up Puzzle Search

Divide the group into two teams. Choose two puzzles with the same number of pieces. To make it easier to decide which puzzle pieces go in the right box when the game is over, mark the back pieces of each puzzle **IN ADVANCE** with a different colored crayon (e.g., the backside pieces of one puzzle are marked with red, the other black). Hide the pieces in advance or let each team hide one set of puzzle pieces for the other team to find. To make it less confusing, choose only one room per team to hide the puzzle pieces. When you give the signal, **see which team can find and assemble their puzzle the fastest**.

Crazy Clues

To make this "**favor find**" **backwards**, give the children a list of where the favors are hidden. Then let them decode a set of clues in order to determine where to look first, second, etc. All clues should be simple sentences written in a backwards style such as **KOOL NO POT FO EHT DEB** ("look on top of the bed") or just a single word clue as **ONAIP** ("piano").

◦ OR ◦

Divide the group into two teams. Whisper to each team where the favors are hidden for the other team. Assign an adult to help each team write clues for the members of the opposite team to read (**written in "backwards" lettering, of course!**).

◦ ALSO ◦

Teams may also need some help in placing clues in the right locations that will correctly match the "backwards" clues. When ready, each team presents the other with a set of clues. See **which team can be first to decipher the clues and locate the treasure.** Let the "backwards" favor find begin!

Musical Madness

Play a new "backwards" version of the old party favorite, MUSICAL CHAIRS! Begin by having everyone sit in a large circle. Two children begin the game by standing together in the center of the circle, a chair placed between them.

The game takes a "backwards" twist as the first two players begin walking "backwards" counterclockwise in a circle around the chair (at this time no music is played). When the music does suddenly begin to **PLAY**, both children must try to sit down in the chair. Whoever is left standing chooses a **new** person and a **new** chair and joins the game so three children begin silently walking in a "backwards" circle around **two** chairs.

Whenever the music **PLAYS**, all the children must try to sit down in a chair. The one child left standing chooses a **new** person and a **new** chair to begin another round until all the children have had a chance to play.

Back To Back Easels

Pin a blank piece of white paper to each child's back. Give each child a dark-colored crayon. Explain that when a signal is given, everyone must **choose another child to be the "back" easel** and begin drawing on the sheet of paper but **FIRST PUT THEIR INITIALS AT THE TOP OF THE PICTURE**. Suggest that they draw only one simple object such as a rainbow, airplane, tree, cat, car, house, chair, lamp, etc.

Give them only five seconds, then ask that each child move to another easel. Each "artist" must then try to figure out what the last "artist" has drawn and try to complete the picture. Once a child feels he/she has finished the picture, he/she may sit down. After everyone is finished, remove the pictures and ask the original artists (the initials will identify them) whether the picture turned out to be what they originally intended it to be.

Topsy-Turvy Think Tank

Have everyone sit in a circle. Bring out a box filled with odd, assorted items from around the house (such as a frying pan, a toothbrush, a sponge, a balloon, a paper cup, etc.). Be certain no one has seen the contents. One at a time, hold up each object and give everyone 30 seconds to look at the object in silence. Ask the children to use their imagination and **think of all the things the object COULD BE**. For example, an ordinary wooden spoon could be a magic wand, Captain Hook's peg leg, a guitar with no strings, a "squished" hammer, a paddle for a tiny boat . . . the crazier the ideas, the better.

After 30 seconds, **begin to pass a deck of cards around the circle as fast as possible**. When a child is ready to say his idea, he/she may take a card from the deck. See who can collect the most cards in one minute. There may be lots of winners each time you play the game. You will be absolutely amazed at what imaginative things the children will say!

Back & Forth Touch It

Divide all the children into two teams. Have everyone stand behind a taped line facing in one direction with their toes on the line. Assign every child a number.

Place four objects in the center of the room such as a brush, book, banana, and a balloon. The leader then yells out, "Number 2, touch the brush!" Or **says each command backwards**, such as "Brush the touch, 2 Number!" Both Number 2's from each team rush to the object, trying to touch the object first (no grabbing or squabbling allowed!). The first to touch the object wins a point for their team. The leader then calls another number and object to touch while keeping score of team points. **"Touch It" can easily be moved out of the house by simply choosing objects from the out-of-doors**.

To add a "backwards twist," ask the children to walk, hop or crawl <u>backwards</u> when going to touch an object. For smaller groups, **blindfold all team members** so they must first find their way to the center of the room and "feel" an object before identifying it and claiming a point for their team.

Nutty Home Video

Film the children acting out a story or just being themselves at the party, then **show the same video in reverse**. The children may even want to act out the highlights of a favorite movie, television show or story and then watch (and laugh) at a **backwards** version. Older children might want to "direct" and do the filming themselves. This activity can also help "direct" the energies of an active group!

Favors

Please Note: Since favors are normally given to birthday party guests as they **leave** a birthday party, remember to give your favor items to guests as they **arrive** at the party.

One example of a "**BACKWARDS FAVOR**" would be to present each guest with a **favor bag turned inside out with nothing inside**. On the outside of the bag, taped to the bottom, would be a gift certificate for a free ice cream cone or yogurt from a local store. Or, any type of small item could be taped to the bottom of the bag such as an eraser, separate sticks of gum, special stickers, candy, etc.

◦ OR ◦

Give each guest a piece of blank paper and some colored pencils or crayons. Group everyone by two's and have each pair of children **DRAW A PICTURE OF EACH OTHER**. When finished, collect the papers, shuffle them and then hold up each picture, letting everyone guess whose face is featured in the drawing. Hand out strips of cardboard or poster board and have each child make a narrow "frame" by pasting the strips around the edge of the picture . . . but first, **turn the picture upside down!** Let everyone take home their colored pencils or crayons as favors.

Duckles to the rescue.....

DUCKLES EGG-STRA EASY ENTERTAINMENT

Large Group Activities - All Ages

When children outnumber adults at a function, the adults in charge sometimes feel a sense of anxiety. This anxiety results from the thought of entertaining a multitude of energetic youngsters.

The question asked frequently by adults at school or church functions, classroom parties, youth group gatherings, office picnics or family reunions is: **How can we keep a large group of children entertained?** Particularly challenging is selecting games that will **invite active participation by CHILDREN OF ALL AGES**. For these large group activities, adult leaders are often in need of **instant ideas** that require few props and little preparation.

This section of the book is designed to suggest easy activities that can be enjoyed by **children ranging in age from four to ten years of age and older** (even adults!). Many games are deliberately active in nature to direct high energy levels in positive directions. Variations that make a game more suitable for young children (ages four to six years) are listed when appropriate.

The Paper Chase

Divide the group into partners and give each couple two pages of a newspaper. Mark a FINISH LINE at the other side of the room, approximately 50 to 60 feet away. Once the starting signal is given, partner #1 places one newspaper page in front of partner #2 who must step on it and **remain standing on one foot until partner #1 places <u>another</u> page down**. In this manner partner #2 moves forward one foot on a page at a time. Once crossing the FINISH LINE, the roles are reversed and partner #2 lays down the newspaper while partner #1 steps from page to page. The partners who finish first, wins. Keep playing . . . even if the newspaper rips!

VARIATION FOR YOUNGER CHILDREN: Each time a page is placed in front of a partner, the child can **jump on it with both feet rather than stand and balance on one foot**. Another idea is to **pair a child with his/her parent** (or older sibling) and have the parent (or sibling) place the newspaper down for the younger child to jump upon with both feet.

Pizza Plop

Save the cardboard rounds from pizza pies or cut out circular shapes approximately nine inches in diameter. **Pretend the circles are pizzas** or have the children color each round to look like their favorite type of pizza. Place the pizza rounds about three or feet apart in irregular,zigzagged lines across the floor (one line of pizzas for each team).

Divide the group into teams to stand behind a taped starting line. At the starting signal, the first team member from each team begins **jumping from pizza to pizza, trying to reach the opposite end of the room without missing a pizza**. If a player should miss "plopping down" on a pizza, he/she must go back to the starting line and try again. The first team to get all their "pizza ploppers" across the room, wins.

VARIATION FOR YOUNGER CHILDREN: Place the pizzas closer together and if a child misses one, just have him/her jump onto the next rather than return to the back of the line.

Blind Racehorses

The children are divided into pairs. **One child is the blind racehorse** and must wear a large paper grocery sack over his/her head. **The other child is the driver** and must instruct the "horse" where to go by touching the "horse" on the right shoulder to go right, on the left shoulder to go left and on the top of the head to go straight ahead.

With tape or chalk, **mark a twisted course that each pair must follow**. At the signal, the drivers begin directing their horses down the course. Neither the horses nor the drivers are allowed to run but a fast trot is acceptable. The first couple to complete the course is declared the winner.

VARIATION FOR YOUNGER CHILDREN: Make a straighter course for horses and drivers to follow with all turns at right angles. **Review the drivers' instructions to their horses several times** so that everyone understands what each signal means. Encourage both horse and driver to move at a slow gait at all times. If time allows, make a horse's tail from strips of paper or yarn and attach to a belt around the child's waist.

Towel Toss

Everyone in the group forms a large circle. There may even be two circles if you have an especially large party. One player is chosen to be **IT** and must stand in the middle of the circle.

A bath towel is knotted once and thrown around the circle, the **players trying to keep the towel from dropping into the hands of IT**. If **IT** manages to catch the towel in mid air, the player who threw the towel becomes **IT**. If a player holds the towel too long, **IT** may grab the towel from the player's hands and the player must then switch places with **IT**.

VARIATION FOR YOUNGER CHILDREN: **Place less children in each circle**. If the circle is smaller, **IT** will have a greater chance of catching the towel. A large beach ball can be used instead of a knotted towel. Also, the children could sit cross-legged in a circle and roll a smaller ball to each other, seeing if **IT** can touch the ball or scoop it up into a plastic bowl.

Balloon Bottle Relays

Place a series of plastic liter soda bottles in two or more straight lines spaced approximately three or four feet from each other. Weight down the bottles by filling them with sand and tie helium balloons to each bottle for an added air of festivity. If indoors, tape down a row of colorful balloons as the markers.

Choose teams and have the players **weave their way through the markers**. Here are a variety of relay ideas: **1)** Push or kick a large, inflatable beach ball around the markers; **2)** Issue brooms so that each team must sweep a small rubber ball through the markers; **3)** Move through the markers carrying a lemon, potato or egg on a spoon; **4)** Balance a book on one's head; **5)** Walk backwards, hop on one leg, jump or crawl.

VARIATION FOR YOUNGER CHILDREN: Attach inflated balloons to the necks of plastic liter soda bottles. In a relay, have the children **jump over each "balloon bottle**," saying the color of the balloon or counting each balloon as they jump over it. Also, tie helium balloons on long strings to the bottles and let the children gently bat at them as they run through the markers.

Tablecloth Tag

All the children stand in a large circle (two circles if your group is especially large in size). Someone is chosen to be **IT** and is **handed an old tablecloth** (card table size works well). **IT** quietly walks around the outside of the circle and when ready, drops the tablecloth behind a particular child. That child must quickly pick up the tablecloth and run after **IT**, trying to touch **IT** with the tablecloth before **IT** reaches the empty place in the circle. If the child doesn't succeed, he or she becomes **IT**.

Hot Air Balloon Blow

Divide the group into two or more teams. Each team stands behind a line marked off with masking tape. Hand the first person in each line a balloon. At the signal, the first person in each team must get down on his/her knees and **blow the balloon until it crosses a taped finish line at the other side of the room. The balloon must then be blown back across the room**. Each team member can take a turn at blowing the balloon across the room and back. The first team with all its members completing the race, wins.

Modern Day Medieval Madness

Remember the days of knights in armor who fought with lances while riding their trusty steed? This game is a far cry from that era as modern day **children can now "joust" with soup spoons and lemons** (or oranges)!

Divide the party into two teams and let each team decide on a name for their "knights." Two players representing each team (or castle) step forward to do battle. Each player holds two soup spoons, one spoon holding the lemon. When given the signal, the "knights" circle each other, trying to topple the other player's lemon while defending his/her own lemon from being toppled by his/her opponent. Only spoons can touch spoons, never an opponent's skin. Set a time limit of one minute for each match. If you have a large group, split the group into smaller circles and have several jousting matches going on at the same time.

VARIATION FOR YOUNGER CHILDREN: Have two adults demonstrate how to "joust" with only the spoons touching each other. Use marshmallows instead of lemons in the soup spoons.

Crabs Creep – Frogs Leap Relay

Divide the children into several teams. Tape off a starting line and finish line. At the signal, each teams sends one member on all fours **walking as a crab** (a position that requires using all fours with stomachs facing skyward and backs parallel to the floor) from the start to finish line. On the return to the starting line, the players must **hop like a frog**. If there is a team of older children, they must also balance a book on their stomach while walking as a crab. If the book falls off, they must return to the starting line again.

Each frog who returns to the starting line tags the next player and the relay continues until **every player has taken a turn creeping and hopping**.

Team Challenge Charades

Divide the group into smaller teams of six to ten players each. Issue each team member a slip of paper. After consulting with fellow team members, each player writes a word on the paper and places it in a team box or envelope. Taking turns, a player from Team #1 takes a charade paper from Team #2's box and tries to **act it out for his/her own team to guess within five minutes**. If the team cannot guess the charade within the time limit, then the other team receives a point. An adult should monitor each group and keep track of all points.

This activity can easily be adapted to the theme of a party or a general category (e.g., ask teams to think of words pertaining to Valentine's Day, Halloween, Christmas, Hanukkah, famous movies, popular television shows, current events, sports figures, etc.).

VARIATION FOR YOUNGER CHILDREN: Allow more time to guess each charade and suggest categories such as colors, farm and zoo animals, favorite foods, etc. Have adults available to write out and translate the name of the charade. See **CHILDREN'S CHARADES**, p. 39, for more ideas.

Sack Charades

This game is a variation of traditional CHARADES. Everyone sits in a large circle. A large bag or box is placed in the center of the circle and filled with a variety of household items. An adult leader acts as the timer. Before the game begins, hand each player a piece of paper, a pencil and 20 wrapped candies.

One at a time, each person in the circle steps to the center of the circle. At that time everyone else writes down how long it will take the group to guess the charade. The adult leader then shows an item **only** to the person acting out the charade. The items in the bag can be as common as a toothpick, penny, jar lid, pencil, paper clip, paper cup, fork, can opener, necktie, stuffed animal, toothbrush, masking tape, key, etc. The timer is set and the player begins acting out **what the object is or what it can do** (a definite challenge!). Whoever guesses closest to the correct time collects one candy from each player.

VARIATION FOR YOUNGER CHILDREN: An adult should choose objects that are simpler to act out (e.g., a ball, toy train, telephone, drum, paintbrush, balloon, etc.) and offer suggestions on how to pantomime, if needed.

• More Activities •
To Entertain Large Groups - All Ages

Duckles to the rescue.....

DUCKLES EGG-STRA EASY EATS & TREATS

Cooking & Crafts Recipes

• Playful Playdough •

featured in the "Pretend to Be" Party

Place the following ingredients in a pan over medium heat:

1	cup flour	1 tablespoon	salad or vegetable oil
1/2	cup salt	2 teaspoons	cream of tartar
1	cup water		food coloring (optional)

Stir the mixture until a ball begins to form. When this happens, remove the pan from the heat and store the mixture in an airtight container. Keep the container in the refrigerator to keep its freshness for a period of time. Should you want to make extra batches of playdough in advance (maybe in a variety of colors), simply pop them in your freezer and allow a day to thaw!

• Yummy Gummy Playdough •

featured in the "Pretend to Be" Party

Mix together one jar of 100% natural peanut butter with one jar of marshmallow cream until it reaches the consistency of your choice (this recipe usually works best if more peanut butter is added to the mixture than marshmallow cream).

Raisins, vegetable sticks, red hot candies, coconuts and chocolate chips can be used to decorate all the imaginative shapes the children can create such as snakes, cars, balls, clown faces, spiders, snowmen, pizza, etc., etc. Now for the best part . . . ALL THEIR CREATIONS CAN LATER BE EATEN!

• Caramel Crunchies •

featured in the "Bubbles, Balls & Balloons" Party

1/2	cup	light corn syrup
1	cup	brown sugar
1/4	cup	butter or margarine
2/3	cup	sweetened condensed milk (approx. 1/2 of a 15 oz. can)
1/2	teaspoon	vanilla
5	quarts	popped corn

Combine butter, sugar and corn syrup in a saucepan. Bring the mixture to a boil over medium heat while stirring frequently. Add condensed milk and simmer, stirring constantly, until mixture reaches a soft ball consistency (from 235 degrees to 237 degrees). Add vanilla. Pour the mixture over the popped corn and stir until well coated. Lightly butter your hands and shape the popcorn into balls. Makes approximately 15 balls about 3 or 4 inches in diameter. After the popcorn balls have cooled completely, wrap each one in colorful cellophane and decorate with stickers or ribbon.

• Bubble Brew •

featured in the "Bubbles, Balls & Balloons" Party and the "Meant To Be Messy" Party

Mix 2 cups of dishwashing liquid (Joy works well) with 6 cups of water and 3/4 cup light Karo syrup. Scrape any excess foam off the solution with a stiff card. When you dip an object into the solution, move it slowly through the air or blow it slowly in order to create the biggest bubbles. Any excess bubble solution keeps well in a covered container.

• "Beary" Punch •

featured in the "Bring Your Own Bear" Party

Fill a clear plastic glass halfway with raspberry or cranberry juice. Add 1/3 cup raspberry sherbet. Fill the the rest of the glass with chilled lemon-lime soda or club soda. Put a cherry or fresh strawberry on top of each glass, place in a straw and serve immediately. Tasty!

• Yogurt "Yummies" •

featured in the "Meant To Be Messy"Party

Place the following ingredients into an electric blender:

1/2	cup	plain yogurt
1/4	cup	powdered milk
3	ounces	frozen orange juice concentrate
1		banana
1/2	cup	water

Blend the ingredients until they are a smooth consistency. Pour into popsicle-shaped forms and freeze. If you use paper cups, pour in the mixture, cover with foil and then push a wooden popsicle stick through the foil. You can make other flavorful varieties of these "Yummies" by using different juice concentrates and fruits. This recipe will make eight popsicle forms or six to eight cups, depending upon how much mixture is added to each cup.

• Paint Without A Taint •

featured in "Meant To Be Messy" Party

Combine 1 cup clear liquid detergent with 2/3 cup powdered tempera paint. If you find this mixture does not provide enough paint for your purposes, increase the measurement accordingly; for example, mix 2 cups of liquid detergent to 1 1/3 cups powdered tempera paint.

Since this "magical" combination of paint and detergent makes paint "easier" to remove from children's clothing, maybe parents will be more willing to provide paper and space for little artists to experiment. Pre-mixed paint can be stored in sealed jars (baby food jars work perfectly!).

• Cannonball Punch •

featured in the "Pirate Treasure Hunt" Party

Choose a favorite melon and scoop enough melon "cannonballs" to fill three measuring cups. These can be made in advance and frozen until the day of the party. Just remember to remove the frozen melon cannonballs at least 30 minutes before you serve the punch.

On party day, mix together one 46-ounce can of your child's favorite fruit punch with one 6-ounce can of frozen lemonade concentrate and two 6-ounce cans of water (use the lemonade can to measure the water). Pour into a punch bowl. Add the thawed melon balls, stir and enjoy!

• Liquid Lava Punch •

featured in the "Dinosaur Dig" Party

This punch is easy to make and, with a stretch of imagination, it does resemble "liquid lava." First, fill your blender with ice cubes. Pour cranberry juice over the ice, stopping when the liquid has filled the blender to within 1 1/2 inches of the rim. Replace the lid and blend the mixture until the ice is "slushy" in consistency (approximately 20 seconds on a high setting).

Turn the punch into "smoking hot" lava by adding dry ice to the punch bowl. Dim the lights, and serve LIQUID LAVA from your prehistoric "kitchen cave."

• Cookie Party Paint •

featured in the "Do-It-Yourself" Party

Combine in a mixing bowl:	2	cups	sifted confectioners sugar
	1/4	cup	milk
	1/4	cup	light corn syrup

Blend the above ingredients together until the mixture is smooth. If you make it in advance, store "paint" in airtight containers until ready to use. On party day, divide up the mixture into separate muffin tins or paper cups and tint with different food colorings. Use small art brushes to paint your cookies with any design you wish. The "paint" will dry to a shiny gloss in about 30 minutes.

• Artsy Art Dough •

featured in the "Do-It-Yourself" Party

Combine in a mixing bowl:	1/2	cup	cornstarch
	3/4	cup	flour
	1/2	cup	salt in a bowl
			food coloring (optional)

Slowly add warm water to the dry ingredients. Knead the dough until it is stiff. You can also add food coloring to tint the dough different colors. If the dough is too sticky to handle, dust your hands with flour. Mold the dough into any shape. If left overnight, it will harden and can then be painted by your child.

ACTIVITY INDEX

AGES ONE TO THREE YEARS

ACTIVITY INDEX

AGES ONE TO THREE YEARS

ACTIVITY INDEX

AGES FOUR TO SIX YEARS

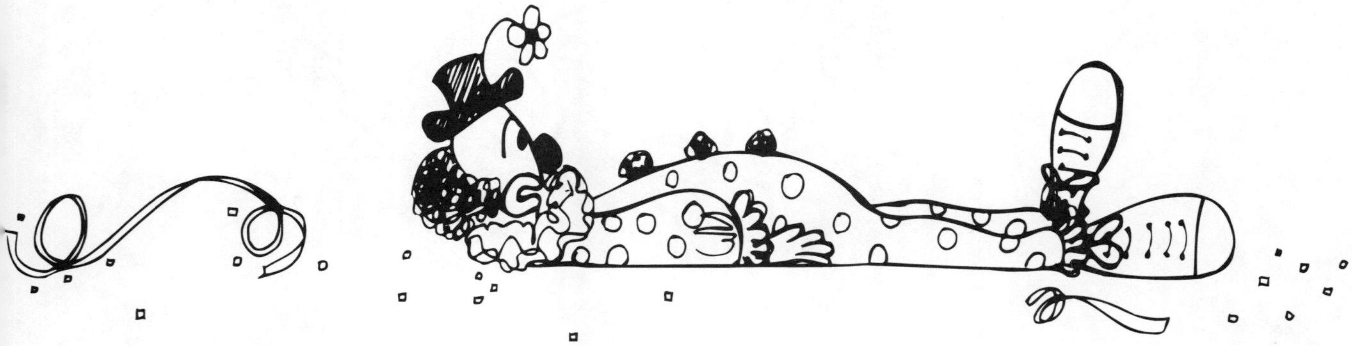

ACTIVITY INDEX

AGES FOUR TO SIX YEARS

ACTIVITY INDEX

AGES SIX TO EIGHT YEARS

ACTIVITY INDEX

AGES SIX TO EIGHT YEARS

About The Author . . .

"Sometimes the best celebrations are ones without a reason."
Dale "Duckles" Reinhard

Dale Reinhard developed many of the party ideas contained in **SIMPLY CELEBRATING CHILDREN** while performing as **DUCKLES the Clown** for children's parties. She has witnessed the magic a clown, and children's parties, can instantly create. It is her hope that this book will make it easy for adults to celebrate children, not only on birthdays, but all through the year. Dale writes for her local newspaper and keeps involved in school and community activities with her husband and two children. She wrote this book at the suggestion of parents and teachers who enjoyed her parties and attended her workshop, "Birthday Party Panic." A graduate of the University of Texas at El Paso, she has given numerous lectures to parents and teachers on "Creative Education - A Learning Journey."

Buy

SIMPLY CELEBRATING CHILDREN

at your local bookstore

• • • • • •

also order toll-free by calling:

1 - 800 - 523 - DUCK

Surprise Your Child With A
DOODLIN' WITH DUCKLES Coloring Book
filled with many of the fun illustrations in this book

PLUS + + + + +

DUCKLES THE CLOWN will send your child a personalized birthday card

Group discounts are available.
For information, call our toll-free number.

AND • • • • • •

The cost is only $3.00 per child. Send in the coupon at least 14 days before your child's birthday. Write information for additional children on the back of the coupon below.

Pressed Duck Publishing
P. O. Box 160931
Sacramento, California 95816-0931

Please send me _______ copies of **SIMPLY CELEBRATING CHILDREN** at $12.95 each. I am enclosing $__________. Add additional $1.50 per book for shipping costs and $3.00 for the DUCKLES personalized birthday card and coloring book (see above). California residents add sales tax. Send check or money order - no cash or C.O.D.'s. Prices are subject to change.

Name ______________________________
(Please Print)

Address ______________________________

City ______________ State ______________ Zip ______________

Quantity of Books	Price @ $12.95 ea.	Total
Duckles Coloring Book & Birthday Card, add $3.00 per child		
Shipping & Handling, add $1.50 per book		
California Delivery, add sales tax		
Total Amount		

DATE OF CHILD'S BIRTHDAY ______________________ **AGE OF CHILD** ______________

NAME OF CHILD ______________ **ADDRESS** ______________________

SPECIAL INTERESTS OF CHILD ______________________

Written in loving memory of

Ma Mabel
Grandma Elsie
Uncle John
Aunt Ruth
Kitty
Nana
Granfer